BFI Film Classics

The BFI Film Classics series introduces, interprets and celebrates landmarks of world cinema. Each volume offers an argument for the film's 'classic' status, together with discussion of its production and reception history, its place within a genre or national cinema, an account of its technical and aesthetic importance, and in many cases, the author's personal response to the film.

For a full list of titles in the series, please visit
https://www.bloomsbury.com/uk/series/bfi-film-classics/

T0346849

'There was surely nothing in the world like red shoes!' (Photograph by Russell Westwood)

The Red Shoes

Pamela Hutchinson

THE BRITISH FILM INSTITUTE
Bloomsbury Publishing Plc
50 Bedford Square, London, WC1B 3DP, UK
1385 Broadway, New York, NY 10018, USA
29 Earlsfort Terrace, Dublin 2, Ireland

BLOOMSBURY is a trademark of Bloomsbury Publishing Plc

First published in Great Britain 2023 by Bloomsbury
Reprinted 2024
on behalf of the
British Film Institute
21 Stephen Street, London W1T 1LN
www.bfi.org.uk

The BFI is the lead organisation for film in the UK and the distributor of Lottery funds for film.
Our mission is to ensure that film is central to our cultural life, in particular by supporting and
nurturing the next generation of filmmakers and audiences. We serve a public role which covers
the cultural, creative and economic aspects of film in the UK.

Cover artwork: © Sam Richwood
Series cover design: Louise Dugdale
Series text design: Ketchup/SE14
Images from *The Red Shoes* (Michael Powell & Emeric Pressburger, 1948), © Independent
Producers; *Oh … Rosalinda!!* (Michael Powell & Emeric Pressburger, 1955), Associated British
Picture Corporation; *Black Narcissus* (Michael Powell & Emeric Pressburger, 1947), © Independent
Producers. Film stills courtesy BFI National Archive

A catalogue record for this book is available from the British Library.

A catalog record for this book is available from the Library of Congress.

ISBN: PB: 978-1-8390-2606-5
        ePDF: 978-1-8390-2608-9
        ePUB: 978-1-8390-2607-2

Produced for Bloomsbury Publishing Plc by Sophie Contento
Printed and bound in Great Britain by Bell & Bain Ltd, Glasgow

To find out more about our authors and books visit www.bloomsbury.com
and sign up for our newsletters.

Contents

Acknowledgments

The making of this book was almost as internationalist and collaborative as the film it celebrates. I am lucky to be able to draw on decades of excellent criticism, and I wish to thank several archives, including Carolyne Bevan and Storm Patterson at BFI National Archive's Special Collections, Anna Meadmore at the Royal Ballet School, Cassie Mey and Javonna Jackson at the Jerome Robbins Dance Division of the New York Public Library, Phil Wickham and James Downs at the Bill Douglas Cinema Museum in Exeter, James Harte at the National Library of Ireland and Rebecca Shawcross at the Northampton Museum and Art Gallery. The writing of this book was generously supported by a work-in-progress grant from the Society of Authors and the Authors' Foundation.

I am grateful for the advice, encouragement, wisdom and generosity of Andrew Moor, Ian Christie, Liz Helfgott, Ruth Barton, Lisa Duffy, James Bell, Nicky Smith, Lawrence Napper, Melanie Selfe, Richard Layne and the discerning community of Powell and Pressburger aficionados. Thanks are due to Rebecca Barden and Veidehi Hans at Bloomsbury and Sophie Contento for inspiration and patience. And to Thelma Schoonmaker for a conversation five years ago about Michael Powell and Rex Ingram. Sorry for steering you off topic.

The book was written in a heatwave summer in Sussex, but also on trains and in airports, hotels and cafés around London, Edinburgh, Riga, Vilnius, Glasgow, Pordenone, Nice and finally Monte-Carlo. I am signing off this note on the terrace of the Café de Paris, where The Archers and the Ballet Lermontov trod before me. It has been an honour to follow their steps, sheathed in satin and soaked in blood, from the footlights to the French Riviera.

Love and gratitude to Nick, who took the corners so well.

1 First Position: 'Put on the red shoes, Vicky'

A pair of red satin ballet slippers, posed *en pointe* in the centre foreground, long ribbons trailing to each side. The Shoemaker who placed them there has barely moved his hands out of the frame when The Girl runs towards the camera from the background, her boyfriend behind her. Then the impossible happens: she leaps into the upright shoes. A close-up of the ruby-red shoes, as in a flash the ribbons snake around her legs. Immediately, she begins to move … The 'Dance of the Red Shoes' plays, and The Girl is alone in the spotlight.

* * *

On 1 March 1986, an enormous pair of red ballet slippers was hoisted on to a street corner in New York City, draped over the walls of the Brooklyn Academy of Music. Each shoe weighed at least 250 pounds and was 30 feet long. They were constructed from 50 yards of red vinyl (strong enough to repel bullets, according to the *Wall Street Journal*) and inflated with heated air from an industrial centrifugal fan. Ann Slavit, the artist who designed this installation to brighten the neighbourhood and welcome visitors to the academy, chose the ballet pumps as an homage to *The Red Shoes*, Michael Powell and Emeric Pressburger's Technicolor film of 1948 about the force of the artistic impulse. Gargantuan, glossy and almost cartoonish, Slavit's shoes were still evocative of the elegance and discipline of dance, with their trailing ribbons and blocked toes. Funding for the project came from Freed of London, the Covent Garden shoemaker that has cobbled shoes for some of the world's best ballet dancers, including the gleaming red satin slippers worn by Moira Shearer in the film. It's a highly volatile image. Both inside and outside the world of the film and its fairy-tale inspiration, red shoes are wrapped in a surfeit of meaning and incomparable allure:

The red shoes in The Shoemaker's shop window

both covetable and cruel. As Hans Christian Andersen wrote in the 1845 fairy tale that inspired the film: 'There was surely nothing in the world like red shoes!'[1]

Red shoes are for scarlet women and feet that stray from the path. The seeds of their potently fetishistic, transformative appeal were sown in the middle of the nineteenth century, in Andersen's vicious story of transgressive female vanity, retribution and repentance. In the imagery of red shoes, these themes dance on, across fashion, literature, art, music and especially in cinema. Nowhere more so than in the 1948 film that had a profound influence on the future of commercial and art cinema, and inspired generations of young viewers to crave shoes of their own. *The Red Shoes* is about a ballet dancer who leaps to stardom in a ballet based on the fairy tale, and whose own ambition is punished in a way that is both gruesome and horrifically apt. The story of Victoria Page of the Ballet

Lermontov who dances to stardom in red slippers, is bound up with the fate of Karen, Andersen's pitiful peasant heroine.

Karen is so poor that she walks barefoot in summer and wears wooden clogs that chafe her feet in the winter. As a kindness, the shoemaker's wife stitches shoes for her out of red rags, which she wears to her own mother's funeral. The shoes attract attention, and soon Karen is adopted by a wealthy older lady who buys her new red shoes, cut from the finest leather. Karen is so delighted that she wears her new shoes to church for her confirmation. She is punished for her vanity, not by the disapproving congregation but by the shoes themselves, which are cursed by a mysterious old soldier with a red beard and a crutch. Once Karen dances a few steps, the shoes take control of her feet. They kick the old lady 'horribly', but Karen is unable to take them off. When she wears them to the village ball, leaving her benefactor alone and uncared for, their power increases. The shoes dance on and on – and Karen cannot resist.

All day and all night, Karen dances past the point of exhaustion, travelling for miles. The old lady dies alone. The shoes have moulded themselves to Karen's feet and cannot be removed. Desperate, she asks an executioner to amputate her feet. Henceforth she will use crutches and wear wooden prosthetics, as clumsy as her hated winter clogs. But the shoes, and the bloody stumps of her amputated feet, dance on in front of her eyes, blocking her path to church. At home and sorrowful, she prays and is visited by an angel who offers forgiveness and welcomes her back to worship. Karen's heart finally breaks. 'Her soul flew on a sunbeam to God … and there in heaven was no one to ask her about the red shoes.'

Vicky Page (Moira Shearer) is no peasant. As she perches in a box at the Royal Opera House, accompanied by her titled aunt Lady Neston (Irene Browne), the broderie anglaise trim on her opera gown designed by Jacques Fath and her dinky tiara give her the air of a princess from a child's picture book. Both her outwardly demure behaviour, and the fierce determination it belies, are apparent when she first encounters Boris (Anton Walbrook), director of the

Moira Shearer as Victoria Page: dressed like a picture-book princess

Ballet Lermontov. She accepts that he won't want to see her dance (quickly confessing that she is 'that horror' he was dreading), but she does have a chilling answer to his interrogation, 'Why do you want to dance?' She replies: 'Why do you want to live?' The circularity of the live-to-dance-to-live logic defines her imminent rise and tragic fall, as life imitates art. Boris chooses Vicky to star in his new ballet premiering in Monte-Carlo, based on Andersen's 'The Red Shoes', and she delivers an extraordinary performance, which the film allows us to experience via an extended 17-minute ballet sequence that reveals her subconscious state as she dances. When Vicky falls in love with the ballet's composer Julian (Marius Goring), Boris forces her to choose between her marriage and her career. She chooses the former, but longs to dance again. When she returns to Monte-Carlo to dance *The Red Shoes*, Julian follows her, and, amid the ensuing confrontation, the red ballet slippers on her feet take control of

The red shoes
dance on and on
(Photograph by Baron)

her body, forcing her to dance out of the theatre and leap to her
death. No angelic visitation revives her. She dies from her wounds
as a heartbroken Julian removes her deadly shoes, and Boris, also
distraught, introduces a final performance of the ballet, with a single
spotlight in lieu of its principal dancer.

Vicky, like Karen, desires the red shoes above all other
considerations. Karen breaks the boundaries of her class by leaving
her home to live with a rich family and wearing shoes designed for
a duke's daughter, and she overturns sexual decorum by drawing
attention to her 'delicate and lovely' self with her eye-catching
footwear – even the statues in church bend to look at her when she
enters. Vicky is already above such class considerations, but she
discovers that her own desire to be a great dancer is more powerful

than she imagined, and that to achieve it, she must reject a traditional wifely role, just as Karen neglects to care for her benefactor, choosing the egoistic, selfish life of the artist instead. It doesn't take a Freudian psychologist to understand that Vicky's decision to leave the ballet and marry Julian is akin to Karen's amputation of her feet: a bloodless but agonising castration. She assures her husband Julian that she loves him, but he points to the red slippers on her feet. 'No, you don't. You love only those.'

The film contorts one of the most dangerous connotations of red shoes, which is heavily underlined in the fairy tale, the suggestion of sexual passion and liberation, as represented by the scarlet lipstick[2] in Powell and Pressburger's previous film, *Black Narcissus* (1947). Vicky's romance with Julian is rather wan, but the relationship she chooses instead is her intense entanglement with the imperious director of the ballet, Boris Lermontov, under whose creative authority she can achieve her artistic ambitions. His is a far more seductive proposition. Vicky's sexual feelings and fears are only expressed in the ballet sequence, in which she dances with various men at the fair and later finds herself lost in the red-light district, on the other side of which she encounters monsters. In her waking moments, Vicky's red shoes signal danger, but also desirable discipline. *Black Narcissus* might also remind us that the accumulating flashes of red on-screen evoke the use of the colour in Catholic vestments to signify martyrdom, blood and fire: the Pope wears red shoes. Boris explains to Lady Neston that ballet is his religion.

As Laura Mulvey has crystallised, the red shoes signal both desire and the death drive and 'allow the relationship between the two to be represented'.[3] Vicky, who tells Boris she must dance as much as she must live, must therefore dance until she dies. Morbidity is stitched into the shoes themselves. When Boris outlines the story of Andersen's tale to Julian, who will compose the score, he caresses the chalk-white plaster cast of a ballerina's foot, permanently *en pointe*. An amputated foot, cast from Anna Pavlova, whose own death is referenced in the film's final scene.[4] What happens in the end, asks Julian. 'Oh, in the end, she dies,' snaps Boris.

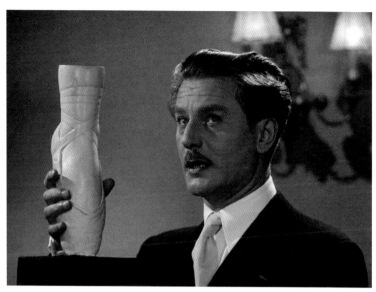
'Oh, in the end, she dies'

In ballet, red shoes carry a more literal meaning. After a performance *en pointe*, ballet dancers are known to discover their flesh-toned shoes are incarnadine from burst blisters, a graphic representation of the exertion required to dance on the tips of your toes. Toe shoes are therefore both like Karen's clogs that make her feet bleed, as well as the leather dancing shoes that look so pretty. The paradox of the ballerina's body is that the appearance of weightlessness and grace involves effort and pain. The effort of dancing *en pointe*, say in the shimmering *bourrée* steps that make the dancer appear to float across the floor, exemplifies Boris's comment that 'a great impression of simplicity can only be achieved by great agony of body and spirit'. Painful for those who have taken the trouble to learn, and impossible for those who haven't. These pains are taken almost exclusively by women. Vaslav Nijinsky, whose tragic story runs right through the history of *The Red Shoes*, is often described as the only male dancer to go *en pointe*, but this is not true.

The paradox of this pose (literary scholar Erin Mackie calls it 'a kind of illusory amputation'[5]) is expressed in Christian Louboutin's absurdly unwearable 2007 Ballerina Ultima shoes. Here an upright ballerina flat is doubled back on an impossibly steep stiletto heel, revealing the designer's signature crimson sole, and evoking high fashion, fetish wear, ballet and the archaic cruelty of foot-binding all at once. The pain and immobility that both *pointe* shoes and Louboutin's parodic pumps represent, call to mind a gruesome memory from another Andersen tale: the stabbing pain experienced by the Little Mermaid when she walks on two legs, the price she pays for savouring mortal love. When *The Red Shoes* was first in pre-production, Powell was greatly impressed by the dancer hired to double for the star in the ballet scenes: 'legs like swords' he wrote in his memoir.[6]

Bloody ballet shoes symbolise more than wounds. They reveal the process. 'Pointe shoes are the central fetish of ballet; they mark

Vicky breaks in the red shoes, while her dresser prepares another pair to be worn

the traumatic origins of every dancer's entry into serious training and her identity as a dancer,'[7] writes Mackie. Blooding one's shoes is a rite of passage for young ballet dancers, and, as dance scholar Mara Mandradjieff writes, a symptom of the process whereby, 'the dancer absorbs the shoes; the shoe absorbs the dancer'.[8] Dancers don't simply put on shoes – the shoes are customised, sometimes aggressively. At the higher levels of ballet, *pointe* shoes are made bespoke for dancers, who often still hand-stitch their own ribbons and elastic to the shoes, to create exactly the right support for their feet and the steps they need to perform. Next, they modify them with hammers and blades, bend, scratch or burn the soles, and darn the toes to provide more strength and grip. In turn the shoes inevitably chafe and deform the dancer's feet. It is a mutual process of breaking-in – a system of attrition masked by the uncanny trick effect in *The Red Shoes*'s transformation scene as Vicky leaps smartly into slippers *en pointe*.

The transformation scene. In a flash ... the red shoes are on

The process may be violent, but as the dancer's foot is supported by the shoe, the shoe moulds to her foot, and the relationship between a dancer and her *pointe* shoe is so intimate that it is true to say that 'the shoes actually know steps – they are shaped by their dancer's performance and body'.[9] Retired dancers may save old shoes, which have absorbed their sweat and 'learned' their favourite steps. After leaving ballet, Vicky yearns for her shoes as more than a symbol of her abandoned dancing career. She wakes up in the middle of the night to caress a pair of dancing slippers: her aspirations and her efforts are encapsulated within these shoes. In the ballet, as The Girl dances in front of the shoe shop, every move brings her back towards the window where she has already seen herself dancing in the red shoes. These shoes are predestined for her feet, and they know the steps of the rest of her life. The Shoemaker poses them rapidly in ballet steps. Flickering light creates the impression that the shoes are shooting out sparks of electricity, and on the score, the use of an electronic instrument, the ondes Martenot, signals that we are entering a fantasy realm. Later, in the film's supernatural ending, Vicky's shoes dance even when she wills them not to.

Vicky's satin pumps are the second most famous pair of enchanted red shoes on film. Just nine years before *The Red Shoes*, designer Gilbert Adrian turned Dorothy Gale's silver slippers ruby red for MGM's extravagant 1939 adaptation of L. Frank Baum's *The Wizard of Oz*. Dorothy's shoes changed colour to take advantage of the Technicolor palette and were dyed a dark crimson to appear bright red on-screen. Audiences of the time will surely have made the mental leap between the two films and their magical footwear. Doubtless, the profitable US re-release of *The Wizard of Oz* in 1949, while *The Red Shoes* was still playing in American cinemas, will have closed the loop. Dorothy's shoes, clicked together three times, carry her home to safety, while the ballet shoes transport Vicky into the enchanted and perilous world of the ballet – her Oz. Ian Christie has described the contrast in terms of Vicky's final choice between domesticity and dance: 'healing magic versus sacrificial magic – you still have to choose'.[10]

The reds of the red shoes are amplified by saturation and repetition. Vicky's violent death and greatest wish are connected by the skeins of red pulled through the film, from The Archers logo to the hues of scarlet lipstick, carnations, theatre curtains, London buses and theatrical greasepaint, even a few stitches on Boris's lapel, that foreshadow both triumph and demise. For Linda Ruth Williams, the colour 'punctuates the story like wounds'.[11] There is a splash, not a flood, of red in almost every frame, accentuated by a contrasting backdrop of blue and yellow tones, exemplified by the coastal French Riviera locations, and the village square décor in the ballet, just as Vicky's auburn hair is set off by the aquatic blue and green palette of her chic resort wardrobe.

On the film's original release, British critics were unsettled by the film's violent ending, which they overwhelmingly nominated

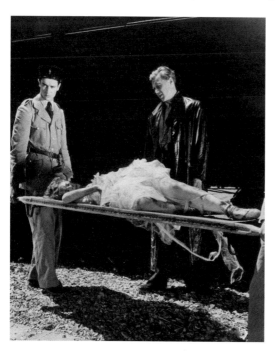

'Lop it off – *please!*' Critics hated the ending (Photograph by Alistair Phillips)

for amputation. 'Lop it off – *please*!' begged one critic,[12] while C. A. Lejeune hoped The Archers would 'make one cut and leave it even better'.[13] The critics took special exception to the use of Technicolor for a death scene, and the vivid splashes of red gore on Vicky's legs after she leaps (or falls?) to her death on to the train tracks. Red, or rather Technicolor, was considered a special effect – and that turned the gore gaudy. In the *Evening Standard*, Milton Shulman questioned the necessity of showing 'the blood-stained body in all its ketchuppish glory', and pleaded: 'Having seen red hair, red shoes and red curtains, did we have to have red blood as well?'[14] These lurid scenes seem unrealistic and coy by the standards of contemporary visual effects, but we can sympathise with this revulsion. Each grisly brushstroke marks the bloody consequences of the fatal, irresistible choice: to put on the red shoes.

* * *

Slavit's giant shoes were deflated and removed just a couple of months after they were installed, but photographs and videos online capture their scale and charm.[15] Back in 1949, making what should have been a more lasting monument, Shearer had imprinted her footprints on the pavement outside the Bijou Theatre on Broadway. When the film finished its record-breaking 110-week run at that venue, a prize was offered for the young woman whose foot would fit, Cinderella-style, into Shearer's delicate step.[16] Sadly, when the cinema was demolished, the concrete slab was removed and its whereabouts are unknown. Closer to the film's source, if you visit the Opéra de Monte-Carlo, you can see Marco Lodola's LED statue of a ballerina, mid-*pirouette*, on the terrace just a few yards from where Vicky makes her fatal leap.

For authenticity, you can visit the Northampton Museum and Art Gallery in England, where a pair of Shearer's red ballet shoes for the film are on display. They are darned and ready to be danced in, but never worn: the satin is richly coloured and shines under its glass case. These beautiful slippers still radiate the potential energy, and the danger, of the dance that once begun, never ends.

2 Overture: The Rabbit in the Hat

Nearly midnight on the terrace of the Café de Paris, and off-screen, a jazz band plays softly. Julian and Vicky meet on the balcony – they are colleagues, not yet lovers. They can't sleep, they're too excited about the future. When the whistle blows, they pause to watch the train rumble past below them, their backs to the camera, as the steam fills the air around them. They wonder what it would be like to be famous and wish each other luck. As she leaves, he whistles a slow, eerie tune, and her foot catches a newspaper trailing in the breeze. Their faces are on the front page.

* * *

Nearly midnight on the terrace of the Café de Paris

'Once upon a time', the familiar opening to many a fairy tale, implies a choice of when and where to start your story. We may begin this biography of *The Red Shoes* wherever, whenever we choose. We will be led by the romance of *The Red Shoes*, which as Julian and Vicky understand on the terrace, resides in the thrill of artistic creation. So, 1845, when Andersen published his bloody tale of shoes and sinfulness? Or further back, in the early 1800s childhood of this most autobiographical of fantasy writers? Andersen, the son of a shoemaker, grew up poor and recalled that, like Karen, at his own confirmation he was preoccupied by his shoes rather than devout thoughts. The audible squeaks stirred his vanity: the congregation would know he was wearing new boots. Two more scraps from his childhood make their way into 'The Red Shoes'. The name Karen was taken from his half-sister Karen Marie. Andersen spent little time with her (she was raised by her paternal grandmother), but her existence haunted him as evidence of what he perceived as his mother's promiscuity. He was more than ashamed; when he became successful, he was terrified that his readers would find out about her. Another formative incident involved his father making a rich lady some dancing shoes – there was a job, and a cottage, riding on her approval.[17] She rejected them and accused the shoemaker of wasting her silk. Furious, Andersen's father slashed the soles with a knife: in that case he would also waste the leather.

We might begin once upon a time in the early 1900s with Pressburger as a boy in Hungary, where 'The Red Shoes' is one of the most popular stories for children. We know he was a keen reader, and devoured Andersen's tales, around the time he was also discovering the magical illusions of early cinema. The first film Pressburger remembered watching was a trick film about a magic plant that grew so tall it smashed through a ceiling. He was eight and entranced enough to puzzle over how the special effect had been conjured: 'I didn't know it was cutting, but I knew something was up.'[18] Similar illusions found their way into Pressburger's work decades later: such as the jump cut that allows Vicky to leap into the red shoes.

We might begin at the Alhambra Theatre in London in 1899, when 'The Red Shoes' first became a ballet – surely its destiny. The production was billed as a 'Grand Spectacular Ballet in Four Tableaux and Five Scenes' based on 'Hans Andersen's Pretty Story' and the tale was transported to Russia, where Karen becomes Darinka, a village girl led astray by the Spirit of Temptation into the theft of 'pretty scarlet shoes' from church. Or in autumn 1935, when Russian-born ballerina Lydia Lopokova (biographer Judith Mackrell describes her as 'guiltily enslaved to her own shoe collection'[19]) chose Andersen's tale to narrate on BBC radio, a performance she repeated for TV three years later.

The 1930s is when the history of the film begins in earnest, but first, let us take a sunny detour to the 1920s and the French Riviera. Michael Powell was here throughout the decade. As a teenager he spent his Easter holidays scrambling around the rocky coastline and getting to grips with the wine cellar at his father's hotel in Saint-Jean-Cap-Ferrat. Powell senior had bought La Voile d'Or on a whim, with the proceeds of one lucky night at the roulette table in Monte-Carlo, and in those Easter trips, he and young Michael motored along the precipitous coast roads to the casino and attended fashionable parties in the grand villas. Later, during location scouting for *The Red Shoes*, publicist Vivienne Knight described how well Powell knew the region, and how recklessly he drove his Bentley: 'Driving with Micky along any road can be pretty devastating, but when he takes the Grande Corniche at sixty describing camera angles with his hands at the same time, you're dicing with death.'[20] In 1925, Powell entered his twenties in the employ of Rex Ingram at his Victorine Studios (another former 'rich man's villa'[21]) in the hills outside Nice. Ingram was a painter as well as a film director and his backgrounds were beautifully composed, his films often fancifully picturesque. The first Ingram film Powell worked on as apprentice was the lavish fantasy drama *Mare Nostrum* (1926), a film infused with Greek mythology, which he later cited as an influence on *The Red Shoes*. *Mare Nostrum* marinated in his imagination alongside the impact of these years spent on the French Riviera, immersed with an international artistic set he called

A young Powell assisting actress Alice Terry at Victorine Studios (Courtesy National Library of Ireland)

'homeless Hollywoodian gipsies'.[22] Ingram continued to be Powell's hero and his friend. Powell visited him in Hollywood when his own career was in a slump, but Ingram had seen *The Red Shoes*, and he gave him a book, inscribed on the title page: 'Am very proud of you. Micky – more power to you. Keep on showing them.'[23] When Powell wrote this scene in his memoirs he burst into tears.[24]

Powell returned to England in 1928, just missing the chance to encounter Pressburger, who, after a period of penury was shortly to start working as a screenwriter at the Ufa studios in Berlin. During his duties he would occasionally be sent down to the Côte d'Azur for well-financed research jaunts. Pressburger later recalled the luxurious novelty of first-class travel, and 'the excitement I felt, looking out of the window waiting to catch sight of my first palm tree. And when I saw it I knew that the hardest period of my life was over.'[25] During the shoot, Pressburger revealed his opinion that the finest view of Monte-Carlo was not from the famous Jardin des Plantes, but the gents at the train station. Pressburger left Germany after the installation of the Nazi regime, and headed for the French film industry, where he wrote a handful of films, including the pan-European affair *My Heart Is Calling* (Carmine Gallone, 1935), shot in English, French and German, starring Polish tenor Jan Kiepura. This backstage drama of romance and overnight stardom among a touring opera company in Monte-Carlo contained early portents of *The Red Shoes*.

The dance world congregated on the Riviera too, in body and spirit. The Ballets Russes had been a revolutionary force in ballet since *The Firebird* in 1910 and the tempestuous premiere of the avant-garde *Le Sacre du printemps* in Paris in 1913 (both composed by Igor Stravinsky). The company, directed by the imperious Sergei Diaghilev, and featuring the legendary Vaslav Nijinsky as lead

Sergei Diaghilev: 'always the most important person in the room' (Sasha/ Hulton Archive/ Getty Images)

danseur, toured internationally throughout the 1910s and 1920s. Under Diaghilev, one of the company's notable productions was *Le Train bleu*, named after the luxury train that travels from Calais via Paris down to the Côte d'Azur, transporting wealthy tourists, often from Britain, between elegant resorts. This one-act ballet was the fruit of a kaleidoscopic collaboration between cutting-edge talents: scenario by Jean Cocteau, costumes by Coco Chanel, décor by Henri Laurens (after Picasso). Diaghilev and Nijinsky were lovers, but when the dancer became engaged to Hungarian aristocrat Romola de Pulszky in 1913, Diaghilev expelled him from the company. Nijinsky's career never recovered and neither did his mental health; he spent three decades in and out of hospitals before he died in 1950.

Vaslav Nijinsky in *L'Après-midi d'un faune*, 1912 (Apic/Getty Images)

Diaghilev wintered on the Riviera and Powell would often spot him in the casino, mingling to charm potential backers of the ballet: 'He was always in control of himself, always the most important person in the room.'[26] When he died in 1929, the company was reborn as Ballets Russes de Monte-Carlo in 1931, resident in Monaco.

Chillingly, those sweeping coastal roads outside Nice were the scene for one of the most gruesome events in twentieth-century dance history. On 14 September 1927, modern dancer Isadora Duncan[27] died when her silk scarf became entangled in the wheel of her car. Some witnesses quoted in American newspapers claimed that her body was thrown from the car in a spectacular upwards movement and she died from the subsequent fall to the pavement. Others that she was decapitated by her scarf.

Although Duncan's death is echoed in the film's tragic finale, it was the controversy surrounding Diaghilev, Nijinsky and the Ballets Russes that would set *The Red Shoes* into motion. So we come to 1934, when the story finally moves to Britain, just before Pressburger crossed the Channel. As the curtains pull back, the baton is lifted by two of Pressburger's fellow Hungarian émigrés: film producer Alexander Korda, who had recently achieved success directing *The Private Life of Henry VIII* (1933), and Romola Nijinsky, who had just published a biography of her husband, which covered his expulsion from the company. Some argue that Korda bought the rights to Romola's book purely to help a fellow Hungarian, but nevertheless, an announcement in the trade press in June 1934 stated that Korda was set to direct 'Paul Muni as Nijinsky and Charles Laughton as Diaghelev [*sic*] in a filmization of the Nijinsky biography'. This never happened, and the rights reverted to Romola, but three years later, Korda saw the possibility of revisiting the idea as a Technicolor star vehicle for his discovery and lover, Merle Oberon.

Ballet was increasingly popular, and the idea had legs. In April 1937 another trade ad revealed that a film known variously as 'The Tempest Within' and 'The Ballet Story' would be the first fruit of a production company formed by Korda and German screenwriter

Günther Stapenhorst. Ludwig Berger, a German film-maker with a flair for musicals, was to direct, while Oberon prepared by taking *barre* classes and Ballets Russes alumnus Anton Dolin, principal *danseur* of the Vic-Wells Ballet, was hired as choreographer and began screen-testing dancers. Korda commissioned a scenario from novelist G. B. Stern and the surviving copy, titled *A Pair of Red Shoes*, is a fairly outlandish concoction of national types and movie musical tropes. It is set during an American tour of the 'Ballet Russe' [*sic*], led by 'Sergei Serbenchieff, the Diaghlieff [*sic*] of the outfit'[28] who is enraged because his best dancers have absconded to the Monte-Carlo Ballet. He is left with Anna Karlova, a past-it ballerina with a vicious ego, and her ingénue ward, Natascha O'Brien, who dances Columbine in a mask under her guardian's name. Scandal, disaster and bankruptcy await

Merle Oberon was set to star in Alexander Korda's ballet film

the company, but Natascha escapes to find success on the vaudeville circuit. The story concludes with Serbenchieff directing O'Brien and her hoofer boyfriend Bricktop Buckley in a New York music-hall production of 'The Red Shoes'. Anna plays the witch and Natascha the heroine, while Bricktop sways gently in the background playing a tree ('Art is Long and Time is Fleeting and every true artist must begin at the bottom,' Serbenchieff explains). Stern does get to the heart of the link between the fairy tale and the ballerina's ambition though: 'Those little girls could no more stop dancing than they could stop breathing, only their kind of dancing is Art, whether done on the Metropolitan Stage or in a cellar in Greenwich Village.'

This is when Pressburger first enters the stage. As he had worked closely with Stapenhorst at Ufa, he was brought in as a consultant of sorts, to read Stern's screenplay, and to offer advice and possibly a rewrite. However, Korda was easily distracted and the story was shelved until early in 1939, when he returned to Britain from Hollywood, where Oberon had been making *Wuthering Heights* (William Wyler, 1939). The couple had just got married in Antibes and Korda was once again inspired to show off his beautiful new wife in Technicolor and *pointe* shoes. Stern refashioned her screenplay, calling the heroine Merle, but to no avail. Korda called in at least three more writers before finally contacting Pressburger, whom he had recently hired as a contract writer and introduced to Powell, another new hire, for their first fateful collaboration, *The Spy in Black*, starring Conrad Veidt. On 1 May 1939, Korda set Pressburger to work at £60 a week to create an entirely new screenplay from what he described as 'a mess. The story is no longer a ballet story, the dialogue is awful. The characterisation is non-existent … I should throw it away.'[29]

Pressburger's first steps led him to Covent Garden. He was familiar with musical life, having played violin since childhood, and his first job in the film industry was a brief stint in the orchestra of Berlin's Capitol Cinema. Very brief: he failed to practise before arriving and was sacked during his first rehearsal. He sat in on rehearsals of the Ballets Russes, as Michel Fokine led dancers through the steps for

Variations on a Theme of Paganini. Pressburger was there to learn how a dance company worked and worried, how they spoke to each other, or didn't – Hungarian conductor Antal Doráti didn't exchange a single word with his musical-minded countryman. Pressburger's biographer, his grandson Kevin Macdonald, speculates that the themes of this ballet, as Fokine described it, found their way into *The Red Shoes*: a demonic figure who enthrals everyone who crosses his path, a heroine who dances until the point of exhaustion, and a circle of 'evil spirits and horrible shades' taunting another character. The similarities are hard to deny, but what Pressburger intended to absorb was the specific atmosphere of the ballet company, which the film's backstage sequences render as a cross-discipline collective endeavour of artists and technicians, from the principals to the *corps* and orchestra. Remember the deftly choreographed chaos of Vicky and Julian's first introduction to the Ballet Lermontov. The sprawl and confusion are like the buzz of a busy soundstage, or perhaps rather a silent film studio, with several stories noisily being told at once.

Pressburger produced a treatment about a girl who is born to dance and who finds overnight success in a ballet based on

Backstage or soundstage? (Photograph by Alistair Phillips)

'The Red Shoes' but, irrevocably torn between her vocation and her lover, finally kills herself. The dramatic action paused midway for a 15-minute sequence of pure ballet, in which a dancing double, and cinematic illusion, would create the impression that Oberon was a prima ballerina in the making. Despite the change of gender and setting, there are still several similarities to Nijinsky's story, as recounted by his wife.[30] Korda ate it up, and hired playwright-novelist Keith Winter to assist Pressburger with the English dialogue, as he fleshed out this story into a screenplay. For a month, they worked happily, with Winter taking notes one day while Pressburger, who led the process, outlined his vision for each scene and shot. The next day, Winter would read the screenplay back to his collaborator and add in his suggestions, including those crisply British character names: Julian Craster after a town in Northumberland, and Lady Neston after a train station near his sister's house in Cheshire.

Although he was employed on another Korda production, Powell was asked to give his approval for the aforementioned sharp-legged dancer to double for Oberon. He found her attractive enough to hope he could direct the second unit. Meanwhile, according to Powell at least, it emerged that Oberon had been amorous with David Niven during the production of *Wuthering Heights* in Hollywood, which cooled Korda's enthusiasm for investing in her ballet film. Nevertheless, the screenplay was ready in July 1939, but, before it could be produced, war broke out in Europe and Korda returned to Hollywood. That wasn't the end of the ballet film; for the next eight years, Pressburger would continue to ponder *The Red Shoes*.

* * *

The story begins again after the war. Powell and Pressburger were established as The Archers, who had made the glorious run of films that began with *The Life and Death of Colonel Blimp* (1943, henceforth *Blimp*) and were working on *Black Narcissus*. Meanwhile, Powell had seen and become besotted with Disney's animated dance film *Fantasia* (various directors, 1940). Pressburger reminded Powell of the old script, which Korda still owned. Emeric had the text because he had tried to buy the rights back from Korda at the end of 1941. Korda sent him a copy, which Pressburger had retyped with the intention of sending it to Vivien Leigh. Another false start for *The Red Shoes*, and cash-strapped Korda, who had already sunk £7,000 into the project, was disappointed once again.

In 1945, Rank's Independent Producers, where The Archers had made their home, took another stab at negotiating with Korda for the rights, but soon dropped it. Korda pounced on his old idea, sending an excitable telegram to his private secretary:

AM CONVINCED THAT THIS WOULD MAKE FIRST RATE INTERNATIONAL FILM TODAY ... PLEASE DO EVERYTHING POSSIBLE TO GET MADAME NIJINSKY HERE ... ALSO GET IN TOUCH WITH KAY HARRISON[31] AND BOOK FOR LONDON FILMS ONE TECHNICOLOR UNIT FROM MIDDLE OF MARCH FOR AT LEAST ONE YEAR.[32]

Once upon a time ... the story begins again

The enthusiasm of Korda, no longer married to Oberon, was typically short-lived. A year later, on 21 May 1946, The Archers were able to buy the screenplay for £9,000. They planned to produce it in style. Powell read it over and thought the story rather dated, but that it 'had all Emeric's usual charm and ingenuity and rather stronger character drawing than usual'.[33] He delighted in the memories it evoked of his youth on the Côte d'Azur. He was on board, with one condition: 'I'll do it if a dancer plays the part and if we create an original ballet of "The Red Shoes", instead of talking about it.'[34]

Powell's insistence on a genuine ballet dancer (one of what he called his 'olympian decisions'[35]), was far from the only change to Pressburger and Korda's first vision for the film, but it is central to the unique brilliance of *The Red Shoes*. Powell suggested that Pressburger was frightened by the idea. Far from it, he intended that the ballet sequence be a true work of art from the beginning. However, the executives backing the film certainly did not welcome it. A star, or at least a well-known name, would have assured greater success at the box office, and they continued to fight for an actress over a dancer, suggesting Ann Todd at one point while scolding Powell to keep his budget in check. George Archibald of Rank wrote to Tom White of Independent Producers, that *The Red Shoes*'s 'casting problem' was also its 'costing problem',[36] and in another letter stated: 'I don't find Mickey's conceit sublime – I find it megalomaniac.'[37] Regardless, Powell and Pressburger's imaginations took flight. This film, which was set in the 1920s or early 1930s, had no truck with British postwar austerity or cinematic realism. Memories of the French Riviera had seduced the film-makers. Pressburger created something worthy of Ufa's most monumental silents, while Powell leaned towards the painterly fantasies of his mentor Rex Ingram, the example of exceptional collaboration from the Ballets Russes and the concept of the 'composed film', which he had begun to experiment with in *Black Narcissus*. *The Red Shoes* was to be a ballet film like no other before it.

3 *Pas de deux*: Powell and Pressburger

A horrible moment of mutual recognition at the Mercury Theatre.
As Vicky performs *pirouettes* in *Swan Lake*,[38] the camera whips
around as fast as her head does. Her point of view is captured in a
series of whip pans, a blur of stage lights, a glimpse of the crowd,
getting closer and closer, intercut with shots of her head turning. She
stops dancing and one face in the audience is highlighted. It is Boris,
watching her intently, deadly serious, as he appraises her skill. A close-
up of her face: piercing blue eyes in a demonic mask of exaggerated
stage make-up. Boris and Vicky have shared the camera's perspective
between them as well as a portentous flash of their entwined destiny.

* * *

Vicky performs *Swan Lake* at the Mercury

Sometimes it only takes an instant to recognise your perfect partner. The dance of *The Red Shoes* from screenplay to film illustrates the collaboration between the two men who share the renowned billing: 'The entire production Written, Produced and Directed by Michael Powell and Emeric Pressburger.'

The creative dynamic between Powell and Pressburger was a circular collaboration based on distinct aptitudes, shared responsibility and a fortuitous spark between artists of very different temperaments but sympathetic visions. They were brought together by Korda for *The Spy in Black* and made three more war films together before forming production company The Archers in 1943 and embracing a sensibility and aesthetic, an entire conception of cinema, that was uniquely theirs. They were very close. The moment they met, Powell felt he had found his ideal collaborator, whose aptitudes complemented his own:

Emeric Pressburger (left) and Michael Powell (right) on the set of *Oh ... Rosalinda!!* (1955) (Photograph by Ronnie Pilgrim)

a screenwriter with the heart and mind of a novelist, who would be interested in the medium of film, and who would have wonderful ideas, which I would turn into even more wonderful images, and who only used dialogue to make a joke or clarify the plot.[39]

Powell likened their partnership to a 'marriage without sex':[40] a term that calls to mind Boris banning such conventionally romantic bonds among his company. It was an ideal creative relationship, one in which each partner 'will be continually rediscovering himself. His thoughts will be continually turning upward and outwards, never inward.'[41] Theirs was a long marriage: although they separated in the 1950s, two decades later they reunited to write a novelisation of *The Red Shoes*.

Pressburger and Powell made films that captured the magic that had charmed the screenwriter when he watched that film about a gigantic plant as a boy. Powell described the process as preparing nests, 'hoping that a little bit of magic will slide into them'.[42] Think of Vicky climbing the overgrown staircase of the Villa Leopolda in her blue gown – a touch of the *fantastique* that evokes the aesthetic of another fairy-tale film, Jean Cocteau's *La Belle et la bête* (1946), but rendered in sensuous Technicolor, as Vicky prepares to be seduced by a beast (an 'attractive brute'). Powell and Pressburger stepped lightly into the enchanted realm of fairy tales. They shared a taste for the fantastical and otherworldly, for a large universe that encompassed heaven and earth, from the celestial negotiations of *A Matter of Life and Death* (1946, henceforth *AMOLAD*) to the miraculous interventions in the finale of *A Canterbury Tale* (1945), or the ancient curse that charms the love story in *I Know Where I'm Going!* (1944, henceforth *IKWIG*). Their partnership began just before World War II, and their first films were commissioned with propagandic intent, but the Hungarian and the Englishman produced images of Britishness that were both proudly patriotic and generously international: see the military co-operation in *49th Parallel* (1941) and the touching friendship between Roger Livesey's English officer

Vicky at Boris's villa: a touch of the *fantastique* (Photograph by Alistair Phillips)

and Anton Walbrook's German in *Blimp*. Much of their work shares a Romantic belief in the importance of art, which is essential to *The Red Shoes*: the pageant players in *AMOLAD*, the organ music in *A Canterbury Tale*. There is a tangible delight in the spectacular qualities of cinema that recalls the conjuring tricks of early film, and an emphatically poetic use of colour. *The Red Shoes* is the most beautiful example of this, especially in its artistic apotheosis, the extended, painterly ballet sequence, in which design, cinematography, music and dance are exalted. As the years passed and the war too, their work developed a creeping morbidity, including the glue-pot assaults of *A Canterbury Tale*, the lethal whirlpool in *IKWIG*, the operating-table purgatory of *AMOLAD* and the violent madness in *Black Narcissus*. Also of course, the death of Vicky in *The Red Shoes*.

Working solo, Powell would take this to its grisly endpoint in the movie-camera murders of 1959's *Peeping Tom*.

Powell was a model cineaste, who aspired as a young man to be the next D. W. Griffith. He worked his way up from the floor of the movie set until he finally got his hands on the megaphone back in Britain in the era of the 'Quota Quickie': the ambition in his early directorial work is evident, but necessarily curtailed by low budgets, and an assembly-line model of production that saw the same studios in use 24 hours a day and films turned around at punishing speed. Pressburger was the wordsmith by trade and musician by inclination who instinctively saw the structures in both narratives and songs. He moved swiftly from selling short stories to newspapers to drafting scenarios for film studios, which allowed his visual imagination to expand. Yet his career stopped and started as he moved from his native Hungary to Berlin, to Paris, to London, picking up a new language, reinventing the tools of his trade, in each new home.

Powell directs the crowd at Cannes train station (Photograph by Alistair Phillips)

The two men settled into a simpatico method of working together and apart. Pressburger would write the screenplay and Powell would offer his thoughts, then Pressburger would revise. Powell took the lead on the studio floor, but with Pressburger by his side, and they insisted that any decision of importance was made jointly. After a shoot, Powell would head for the hills for a head-clearing hike, while Pressburger stayed close to supervise the editing. Their shared production credit was a tactic to avoid interference and to ensure that the finished film reflected their vision. Powell was outwardly, vocally confident; Pressburger the quiet worrier who only spoke up when he was sure of his point.

It's reductive to call Pressburger the screenwriter and Powell the director. The latter's phrasing is more attractive and more apt. 'I'm not the originator of the story,' he said, 'but I am the teller of the tale.' It may also be fair to say that Powell's director's ego made distinct credits impossible. He wrote:

Pressburger and Powell on location for *The Red Shoes*

Emeric used to say to me that when he started to expound a new idea,
I would come to it, meet it, appropriate it, make it work, and by the time
he had finished explaining it I would be coming to him, explaining it,
improving it and introducing it as my own.[43]

You may want to bear that in mind when you read about the
incident from the production of *The Red Shoes* that Powell claimed
was indicative of their approach. As the end of the film draws near,
Vicky is ready go on stage and she is wearing the red shoes, even
though those aren't the shoes she wears for her entrance. 'Emeric
was the writer and knew that she couldn't possibly be wearing the
Red Shoes when she runs away. I was a director, a storyteller, and
knew that she must.'[44] In fact, he had previously insisted on shooting
Vicky's death scene with the red shoes on Shearer's feet ('I already
had an image in my mind of the shattered body of the ballerina
lying on the railroad track, and her Red Shoes, red with blood'[45]).

Vicky realises that the red shoes are running away with her

An earlier draft of the screenplay includes an awkward line of explanation, but Powell's solution was better. Vicky is shown breaking in the shoes as ballerinas do before a performance. Next ('so much for realism' wrote Powell) cinematographer Jack Cardiff used 'a high intensity of colour and light, which seemed to give the shoes life'.[46] Then Powell gave the direction for Shearer to suddenly stop and turn around to give the impression that the shoes are controlling her. It's a terrifying moment in the film, not just because of Vicky's peril, but because, in common with all the film's most thrilling scenes, realism is abandoned. The laws of cinema as an artform supersede the conventions of realism, and in this realm, anything might happen next. It is only right that the brushstrokes are visible in the gore painted on to Vicky's legs – it follows the tradition of the painted anti-realist sets of German Expressionist cinema. By looking back to the silent era, Powell and Pressburger combined the freedom of animation with the human presence of live-action cinema.

The true genius of this moment is that narrative realism is discarded in favour of the film's unifying symbol, the red shoes. In a discussion of the pair's collaboration on *IKWIG*, Ian Christie identifies how they built a nest for magic: 'how a film-maker who is not working in an avowedly experimental mode can preserve the integrity of simplicity of the originating image, while developing an acceptable narrative'.[47] Here the originating image, the red shoes, must be allowed to run away with the film, regardless of the demands of plot. The brilliance of the Powell and Pressburger partnership was that they allowed that to happen.

* * *

The Archers had a five-point manifesto, crystallised in a letter Pressburger sent to English actress Wendy Hiller, trying to persuade her to appear in *Blimp* (she would eventually lead *IKWIG*).[48] The first two principles referred to The Archers' independence and responsibility for their own work. Evidence for this in *The Red Shoes* is provided by how far Powell and Pressburger exceeded

the budget set by Rank,[49] and their indifference to the executives'
dismayed response to the finished film. *The Red Shoes* was their most
extravagant work: 'At this point in their career, the Archers were tall
in the saddle and pretty arrogant about it,'[50] wrote Powell. Principle
three asserted that 'A real film, from idea to universal release, takes a
year or more,' which was exemplified by this film's long gestation. The
fifth principle was partly to do with respectfulness on set, which may
have been a little shaky at times during this shoot. One strength of the
duo was that Pressburger was a gentle soul, able to soothe the upsets
caused by his partner's quick temper. It was also to do with gathering
a strong team. The Archers comprised artists and technicians of the
highest skill, and, if sometimes they jostled among themselves to
get their ideas across, that was only to the benefit of the film. As the
manifesto says: 'They will fight and intrigue to work on a subject
they feel is urgent and contemporary and fight really hard to avoid
working on a trivial or pointless subject.' The atmosphere on set was
animated by a collective passion for the film's highest ambitions.
Marius Goring remembered that even the electricians were engrossed
in the action, Powell having embraced them by saying their work
was essential to the film: 'Follow what is going on down here and
please make your own suggestions, then we will achieve something
together.'[51] The production of *The Red Shoes* turned Cardiff from
someone who considered ballet 'sissies prancing about',[52] to a fully
paid-up balletomane.[53] Cameraman Christopher Challis recalled that
during the filming of the ballet, the entire crew stayed late each day to
watch the rushes and see Hein Heckroth's designs come to life.

The fourth principle is the most interesting: 'No artist believes in
escapism. And we secretly believe that no audience does.' The escapist
appeal of a fairy-tale drama about a young ballerina finding success in
sun-soaked Monaco would lead the film's marketing. The ballerinas'
elegant wardrobes by Paris designers Jacques Fath and Carven,
Boris's lavish attire (including an ornate embroidered dressing gown
improbably made in less than a week by the in-house designers rather
than purchased in a boutique) and his banquet breakfasts create an

enticing fantasy of plenty for postwar audiences mired in austerity.
But *The Red Shoes* is far more serious in its intentions. While many
of the duo's wartime films had propagandic messages folded within
(*AMOLAD* was intended to promote Anglo-American relations), *The
Red Shoes* is propaganda for art, a second manifesto for a peacetime
indulgence in creativity and excess. In Powell's words: 'We had all
been told for ten years to go out and die for freedom and democracy,
for this and for that, and now that the war was over, *The Red Shoes*
told us to go and die for art.'[54] For Powell and Pressburger, cinema
offered a challenge to the audience. If wartime propaganda asked the
audience what sacrifices they would make for the war effort, *The Red
Shoes* forces the viewer to consider what agonies of body and spirit
they would undergo to create a work of lasting beauty.

* * *

First came the screenplay, and Powell's response to Pressburger's
words. There are copies in the BFI archive of a script dated 1947,
when work began anew on the film. It is billed 'A production of The
Archers/ By Emeric Pressburger and Keith Winter/ From an original
story by Emeric Pressburger'.[55] It's a capacious draft, far more
detailed and complex than the final film – and less inspired. The plot is
to the forefront here, and that is not the film's strength. The meaning
of *The Red Shoes* transcends the narrative of Vicky's overnight success
and her romance with Julian. The ballet sequence is extensive but
is to be filmed in a more conventional style, with cutaways to other
characters, as well as the audience. Before dying violently on stage as
The Girl, Vicky looks to Boris. There is a donkey in the wings, which
must be led away. Its presence was at the mercy of a bet made between
Boris and Sergei: the designer may use the donkey only if, as he
predicts, Vicky fails the challenge of dancing *The Red Shoes*.

    The donkey isn't the only thing that had to go. This draft tends
to over-explain the story. Boris tells Julian: 'Miss Page has put on
the red shoes in more senses than one!' There are more locations
(Rome and Venice), and a Cockney dancer called Lillian Crawley

Sergei doubts Vicky's ability to dance *The Red Shoes* (Photograph by Alistair Phillips)

('a snub-nosed, rather common but essentially vital little thing'), who contrasts with Vicky's genteel sophistication. She introduces the music-hall element of British dance culture, notably in gossip about a dancer who claims to have had her tonsils removed three times – implicitly a cover story for abortions.

There's a class dimension too in the love affair. Julian bursts into the Royal Opera House shouting 'To the Bastille!' and once seated in the section evocatively known as 'the gods', muses on how he'd never be in the stalls unless selling programmes. The theme continues, with Julian and Vicky falling out over her aunt's wealth. 'Are you a Communist?' she asks. 'I don't think so but there are certainly some things that make me see red.' Boris exploits Julian's class-consciousness, commissioning him to score a ballet called *The Fourteenth of July*. Back in England and down on their luck after leaving Lermontov, Vicky and Julian are forced to move from the Savoy to a 'Bayswater boarding house', a milieu she finds 'indescribably sordid'. This class element harks back to the Nijinsky story: Vaslav was born in Kyiv to fairly humble Polish dancer parents, while Romola's parents were illustrious. It also puts the story in the tradition of 1930s ballet melodramas, including *Dance Pretty Lady* (Anthony Asquith, 1931) and *Waterloo Bridge* (James Whale, 1931),[56] in which music-hall ballet dancers are generally working-class girls, perceived as the kind of women who may have had multiple tonsilectomies.

The class-divide drama had to go; it was dated and not well handled, but more importantly, it was too grounded in reality, and detracted from the mythical quality of the story. No film about British people in the 1940s can truly escape class nuance, but *The Red Shoes* is primarily about rootless bohemians gathering together on foreign soil for a shared artistic mission. Class, like marriage and parenthood, is beside the point.[57]

To illustrate how the film moves beyond these concerns, take the scene in which the red shoes are chosen. In the earlier screenplay Vicky chooses the shoes in a 'smart shoe shop in Monte Carlo',[58] accompanied by Boris. This is where he tells her that she will be staying at the Hotel de Paris (where upper-class Vicky has stayed before as a tourist) with the other principals, not with the *corps*. Vicky questions him: '"The Red Shoes" are taking rather a snobbish route, aren't they?' Boris replies with a smile: 'Does that matter, if they know where they are going?' This is replaced in the film by one brief scene with no dialogue: the camera pans down a rack of various red slippers. Sergei and Boris (their heads out of frame) walk down the line as Sergei points at each pair with his paintbrush. A blow of Boris's cane indicates the chosen pair with a thud. And another. Sergei's paintbrush blesses the shoes and a chime shimmers on the soundtrack. Then there is a dissolve into the next scene. So much for realism. A literal scene is replaced by an enchanted moment, one that hovers halfway between realism and the artifice and fantasy of the ballet itself. This tiny scene becomes the bridge between the dreamy

Selecting the red shoes: an enchanted choice

meeting of the lovers and their destiny on the terrace, and the prosaic business of rehearsal. Chime by chime, the film transforms the Côte d'Azur into a fairy-tale realm.

There is one moment in this draft that seems insubstantial on the page, but on-screen might have been Powell and Pressburger at their poetic best. At a monastery where Vicky and Julian stop for a drink on the night when they get lost,[59] there are a pair of tankards reserved for married couples. When the company returns there for lunch, Vicky and Julian see Boris's name in the visitor book and realise that he has been tracking them. A cloud passes in front of the sun, and that's the moment that they decide to get married. The enchantment of the tankards creates a symbolic wedding that happens simultaneously with Boris's jealousy overshadowing their happiness. There is another line in this draft to catch the heartstrings, though – although it could never have stayed. Boris almost declares he is in love with Vicky:

The lovers get lost on the enchanted coast (Photograph by Alistair Phillips)

'I, too, used to think there was no room for anything in my life but work!' But *The Red Shoes* is not about a love triangle.

Pressburger's later draft of the screenplay, in two parts, is closer to the film, with no more Lillian, and a much more streamlined narrative. The ballet sequence has been much more developed, outside of the screenplay. And now it is the break with filmed-ballet convention that Powell envisaged:

We are designing a ballet for film, therefore for a film-audience ... So all objective shots of the audience are <u>out</u>, except as and when seen by Vicky from the stage as she dances: dim figures, strange effects, a beating baton, hypnotic eyes, millions of eyes ... We <u>never</u> see the Theatre de Monte Carlo: we are it, in our stalls at the cinema.[60]

* * *

The film that emerges from this process is unmistakably a Powell and Pressburger movie. It is a significant milestone in the journey of their collaboration, and a technique they pursued idiosyncratically. Powell called it the 'composed film' – in which the musical score is recorded in advance and the action is shot to playback. Officially, he had begun to experiment with this technique on *Black Narcissus*. Powell and composer Brian Easdale arrived on set with stopwatches and timings to shoot a short 'opera', in the sense that 'music, emotion, image and voices all blended together into a new splendid whole'[61] to a pre-recorded piano track. This is the mostly wordless sequence, a supernatural chase, that closes the film, starting at dawn and climaxing with Sister Ruth's (Kathleen Byron) horrific fall from the bell. It's more like five minutes than the 12 Powell claims in his memoir, but it is intensely terrifying cinema, a depiction of a woman driven mad, haunted by her own desires, and lost in a strange world. Much like the *Ballet of The Red Shoes*.

Charles Barr traces the origins of Powell and Pressburger's knack for 'composed cinema' back to the opening minutes of the first film they worked on together, *The Spy in Black*, with its 'high-intensity interaction' of 'image and movement and music'[62] – the performances of Conrad Veidt and Marius Goring are so well

The operatic finale of
Black Narcissus (1947)

synchronised they are almost a dance. Pressburger would have been familiar with the technique, as some of the operetta films he worked on at Ufa in Berlin were shot this way. Powell borrowed the term from Friedrich Feher, a Viennese director who made just such a film, *The Robber Symphony*, in Britain in 1936. Powell never saw it but was impressed by the experimental idea of shooting to playback. For him, the 'composed film' was the perfect film, a pure cinematic art that recalled the fluent expressiveness of silent cinema. This was what he loved so much about *Fantasia* and its lavish animations set to classical music. In many ways, Powell's heart still belonged to the silent era, when three-piece orchestras played in studios and he confessed himself struck by 'a kind of restless ambition, a subconscious desire to experiment, which made me want to reverse the order of things'.[63]

The ballet sequence of *The Red Shoes* was their longest, most ambitious foray into 'composed film' to date, and their greatest success in the form. The combination of opera and dance in *The Tales of Hoffmann* (1951), which was an elaborate 'composed film' from start to finish, tested the endurance of many audiences, with one critic calling it '127 minutes of the hardest filmgoing'.[64] However, the *Ballet of The Red Shoes* achieves a dazzling perfection, entirely appropriate for a film about obsessive genius and the drive for greatness.

Composed film requires a punishing procedure and the ultimate authority of the director on set. Powell recalled shooting the climax of *Black Narcissus* as a triumph: 'It worked! It worked! I have never enjoyed myself so much in my life. For the first time I felt I had control of the film with the authority of the music.'[65] Remember how often Vicky is instructed to submit to the score: 'Nothing matters but the music!' The tension between a producer who desires complete control and a collaborative team with artistic egos of their own would find expression in the fictional Ballet Lermontov, but also in the making of *The Red Shoes* itself.

4 The Company: 'Enough genius in each man or woman'

Boris, the older man with a halting foreign accent, shows young composer Julian a ballet score in need of revision. When Julian sees the title – *The Red Shoes* – inspiration strikes in a heartbeat: a shimmering chord on the soundtrack, and a snatch of a vivacious dance tune. The composer's eyelids flutter. The older man's voice echoes and distorts, then slows to a crawl before Julian wakes from his split-second daydream.

* * *

(Left to right): Anton Walbrook, designer Jacques Fath, Michael Powell, Moira Shearer and Emeric Pressburger discuss costumes

The Red Shoes represents the high peak of The Archers' approach to film-making not just as a collaborative effort but as a multifaceted assemblage of artistic disciplines. The film can be described as a *Gesamtkunstwerk*, a term coined by German philosopher K. F. E. Trahndorff in 1827, and popularised by Richard Wagner to describe the 'total artwork' that incorporates several artforms. Dance critic Arnold Haskell defined ballet as 'the meeting place for all the arts'[66] and Diaghilev's productions at the Ballets Russes exemplify the *Gesamtkunstwerk*. As Léonide Massine wrote in his memoir, they were 'the inevitable results of the collaboration of a number of men who were steeped in European art and culture'.[67] When Massine first joined the company to replace Nijinsky, Diaghilev sent him to museums to understand his 'theories on the fusion of music, dance, drama and painting'.[68] Critic Caryl Brahms wrote of Massine, the summer he shot *The Red Shoes*, that his 'whole history has been one of catching light from his collaborators – musicians, painters, writers and dancers, and of translating their combined vision into movement'.[69]

Pressburger's statement of intent for the film set a benchmark of quality for the ballet sequence, a *Gesamtkunstwerk* of its own:

I was always fascinated by the idea of actually creating and showing a genuine piece of art on the screen. You know how in books and in films you are often told that such and such a person is a genius, or writes wonderfully, or composes extraordinary music – but of course it is always a cheat, the audience is never allowed to see it – because if they did they would see how mediocre it was. But in *The Red Shoes*, I wanted to show the work of art on the screen, so that people would actually say: 'Ah that's what all the fuss is about!'[70]

The Red Shoes does not just present this perfect ballet, but shows us how it was made, betraying its fascination with the why and how, as well as the what of art. There are limited rehearsal scenes, but we are invited into conversations between the company's leading creatives:

The Ballet Lermontov in rehearsal (Photograph by Alistair Phillips)

musical director 'Livy' Montague (Esmond Knight), choreographer Grischa Ljubov (Léonide Massine), designer Sergei Ratov (Albert Bassermann) and Lermontov himself.

In 1946 Sergei Eisenstein wrote that 'cinema is the most international of all the arts ... first of all because with its improving techniques and growing achievement the cinema can establish a direct international contact of creative thought'.[71] The Ballet Lermontov promises a model of how a *Gesamtkunstwerk* is made, as well as this concept of an 'international contact of creative thought'. Uncannily, it also offers a mirror image of the team who brought together *The Red Shoes*, and the clashes and co-operations between them, including cases of life imitating art.

Designer Hein Heckroth valued the process: 'We have here in England the advantage that we are all still individuals who can talk and fight with each other – we are not closed up in departments.'[72] The idea that artistic disciplines should remain separate is mocked in the opening scene of the film, as music students and balletomanes in the opera house remain pompously and exclusively devoted to their own medium. In the Ballet Lermontov, the disciplines do meet, but one decision is final. Analysing the scenes of executive collaboration within the film, both in Boris's villa and in a cut scene set in the Café de Paris, Mark Nicholls describes how the process is not one of collective, joint decision, but of one authoritative leader making decisions that benefit from the competing passions and excellence of the creative team: the 'jealous individuality of the component artists'.[73] A pertinent theme in a film inspired by a tale that concocts a vicious punishment for pride.

The most glaring case of jealous rivalry between artists occurs in the opening scene. Watching the performance of *Heart of Fire*,

Julian storms out of *Heart of Fire* (Photograph by Alistair Phillips)

Julian realises that the composer, Professor Palmer (Austin Trevor), has stolen his work – so he storms out and writes an angry letter to Boris condemning the older man's plagiarism. Waking up in the morning with a cooler head, he regrets his outburst, but it is (conveniently) too late to take it back. Boris has read his letter, and consoles Julian that talent is more important than renown: 'It is worth remembering, that it is much more disheartening to have to steal than to be stolen from.' He won't censure Palmer, but he does hire Julian in a junior role. Julian continues to hustle. He oversteps his bounds by rehearsing the orchestra out of hours and corrects a mistake in one of the stolen passages in *Heart of Fire*.

It's not enough to usurp Palmer's role. When Boris gives him the score for *The Red Shoes*, asking him to rework certain marked passages, Julian completely rewrites everything, confident he can do better. He bursts into Lermontov's conference with his brand-new score, and races out ready to complete the orchestrations.

Julian plays his new score to the inner circle

The approval of his new music is muted but certain: Sergei nods at Boris, Grischa begins to mark time, strolling around the room as he considers choreography, then Livy joins him at the piano, rapt – the music inspires movement. Boris merely tells him to stop playing and get back to work, much to Sergei and Grischa's obvious amusement. Compliments from Boris are often buried or backwards, as when he tells Julian that 'there are passages in *Heart of Fire* which no one need be ashamed of' or reminds Vicky that his confidence in her is not shared by his colleagues. Julian is so fixated on his own success that he needs only the barest encouragement to exceed expectations. Vicky also strives to exceed expectations – she dances 'full out' even in rehearsal, which her partner, who has vastly more professional experience, finds unnecessary. As a measure of their personal perfectionism, Julian and Vicky are stricken by nerves before the performance of *The Red Shoes*, even if Julian tries to deny it. Other members of the group are similarly panicked: Grischa loses the shoes, Sergei frets over a broken door. Only Boris remains serene.

Behind the scenes on *The Red Shoes*, another score was attacked with something stronger than a blue pencil, and another switch made. Polish composer Allan Gray[74] had scored all The Archers' films up to *AMOLAD*.[75] British composer Brian Easdale was hired for *Black Narcissus* as he had some expertise with Indian music, a background in opera and a friendship with the novel's author, Rumer Godden. The Archers asked Gray to compose for *The Red Shoes* but when he finally played his score to the team at his cottage there was an awkward moment. It was not good. Choreographer Robert Helpmann already considered the work-in-progress 'utterly commonplace'[76] but when he heard the final score, he said he would reject it if it were submitted at Covent Garden.

'It was awful – for him, as well as us,' recalled Powell. 'We paid him his fee and called in Brian Easdale.'[77] Time was tight and the new composer asked for a week to complete the score. Six days later, Easdale called The Archers to his flat, and in Powell's memory, it was uncannily like the scene in the film, when Julian plays his revised score for Boris and his team. Just like Boris, Powell asked for the full score 'yesterday'. In the film, there's a nod to the Nijinsky narrative in this subplot as the first score was written on the South American tour, which is where he was fired by Diaghilev. Powell described Easdale as one of his dream collaborators – they bonded instantly – and he was an ally in the pursuit of the 'composed film'. Easdale's composition style was well suited to *The Red Shoes*, combining the influences of late Romanticism with modernism and electronic sounds. His score won one of the film's two Oscars. That night he became the first British composer to take home the Academy Award for Best Original Score.

Heckroth, already present in the inner circle, would win the film's other Oscar, for Best Art Direction, but he too had made a painful entrance. Fellow German Alfred Junge was The Archers' regular designer ('probably the greatest art director that films have

Hein Heckroth at work on designs for *The Red Shoes*

ever known,'[78] said Powell), who hired Heckroth to design costumes
and titles on *AMOLAD* and *Black Narcissus*. Unbeknownst to
Junge, Powell and Pressburger asked Heckroth to work on the
ballet sequence of *The Red Shoes*, having been underwhelmed by
Junge's designs for that section, which didn't travel far enough
in the direction of fantasy. Heckroth was a very different artist, a
painter who had launched himself into the dance world with his
avant-garde designs for Kurt Jooss's apocalyptic ballet *The Green
Table* in 1932; he was interested in surrealism and exploring the
subconscious through design. Powell gave him two notes: one, that
the ballet should be modern dress ('The Red Shoes girl is a girl like
other girls ... there's nothing period about it') and two, 'I don't want
a theatre-ballet, I want a film-ballet.'[79] Heckroth was to reveal what
Vicky is feeling as she dances. After Heckroth had been at work for
a month, Junge discovered this challenge to his authority in his own
department and resigned in anger. Powell merely laughed – he knew
Junge had other options. Heckroth should take over the rest of the

One of Heckroth's designs for the ballet sequence

film, and Arthur Lawson, who had a more practical understanding of set-building, would support him – a much more harmonious collaboration. Powell later described the transition from Junge to Heckroth as a decision 'to get the architect, with his naturalistic conceptions, out of colour film, and get the painter in'.[80]

Heckroth created high-end realist interiors for the film, including the creamy luxury of Lady Neston's London apartment and the ornately decorative spaces commandeered by Lermontov in Monte-Carlo and Paris. The recreation of a room inside the Paris Opera House is spectacular. With its mirrors, crystal chandelier and gilded plasterwork, it is a sumptuous place for a rehearsal. He could work quickly too, apparently painting a backcloth for *Giselle* in 20 minutes. The ballet sequence is Heckroth's masterpiece within *The Red Shoes* though, with a vivid aesthetic composed from transparent fabrics, and pastel colours, which travels from realism, via Expressionism to surrealism and evokes the style of the Ballets Russes. It was built from his designs up, a short 'composed film' based on his own paintings. After the film's release, his designs were exhibited in London and New York.

Heckroth's key collaborators included Jack Cardiff, the cinematographer who brought his appreciation of fine art into his technical work. Veritably born in a trunk, Cardiff was from Great Yarmouth and both his parents were music-hall entertainers. He segued from juvenile stage roles into movie work in the silent era. As a cinematographer, he styled himself the *enfant terrible* of Technicolor, who broke the company's design rules to achieve incandescent, often shocking results. For The Archers, this meant the lusciousness of the earth-bound scenes in *AMOLAD* and the Expressionistic palette of *Black Narcissus*. He appreciated working with Powell, who encouraged his 'wild and experimental' ideas. 'Nothing was too risky for Micky.'[81] For *The Red Shoes*, Cardiff experimented with 'choreophotography': discreet trick shots, travelling mattes, and varying the camera speed, often shooting Shearer at silent-era rates of 18 or 19fps. As he said, 'to interpret the

Jack Cardiff's cinematography transformed Heckroth's oil paintings into cinema (Photograph by George Cannon)

choreography as though the audience was in the theatre, it was quite necessary for the camera to be a little dishonest'.[82] Cardiff oversaw the introduction of a new, super-powered spotlight bright enough to show up against all the other lights on set, a water-cooled arc lamp with 300 amps of power. Two more prototypes known as 'brutes', 225-amp lights with wide beams, also joined his arsenal.

Cardiff spent time making tests of camera speed for the ballet sequences so that the dancers would appear to hover in the air – a suggestion perhaps of Nijinsky's celebrated leaps. He used a technique that allowed him to vary the camera speed in the middle of a shot, just as in his silent days, he would crank a camera more slowly to make the action in a fight scene appear more frenzied. In front of Cardiff's camera, dancers could float, or change tempo midway through a *pirouette*. Collaboration can be about finding balance. Having seen the effect of these strong lights on the painted backdrops, Heckroth had to tone down the colours so they wouldn't overshadow the dancers.

Christopher Challis, another Archers' stalwart and a colour specialist, was the camera operator. By this time he was beginning to work as a cinematographer, but *The Red Shoes* was a challenge he couldn't resist. Reginald Mills returned to edit the film, and George Busby, another regular and a friend of Powell's from the Ingram days, was on board as assistant producer. With this backbone, even a project as ill-starred as *The Red Shoes* had a chance of making it to the cinemas.

The rest of the team were found in Covent Garden rather than Pinewood. Easdale's score would be recorded by the Royal Philharmonic Orchestra, conducted by Thomas Beecham. Australian dancer and actor Robert Helpmann, a former pupil of Massine, was to choreograph the ballet and appear as the company's chief male

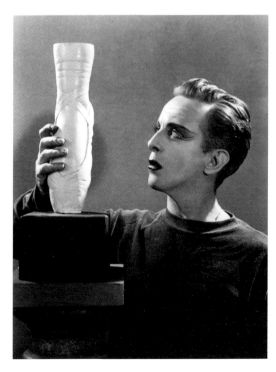

The multitalented Robert Helpmann brought his skills as dancer, actor and choreographer (Photograph by Alistair Phillips)

artiste Ivan Boleslawsky. Shearer recalled that, with filming taking up six days a week, he wrote the ballet on Sundays, which meant she was in the studio rehearsing too. Helpmann had acted for The Archers before, as the cornered Dutch quisling in 1942's *One of Our Aircraft Is Missing*, and would achieve cult fame as the Child Catcher in *Chitty Chitty Bang Bang* (Ken Hughes, 1968), but it was this film he enjoyed making the most. To give an indication of the breadth of Helpmann's talent, his straight acting credits included an acclaimed *Hamlet* at the Old Vic in 1944. Far from fearsome on set, Helpmann was remarked on as the kindest and most generous collaborator, which you can infer from his understated performance in the ballet – his role is to partner The Girl, not to call attention to his own steps. Russian Massine played his counterpart on film, the exuberant ballet master and choreographer Grischa Ljubov, as well as dancing The Shoemaker in the ballet. If there was jealousy between these two dancer-choreographers it mostly expressed itself in a little teasing about the age difference: Helpmann was 36 and Massine 50. Massine was reluctant to join the film at first, having, as he wrote in his memoir,

found the cinema unsatisfactory as a medium for choreographic composition. But after discussing the matter with Powell at some length, I decided that the charm of Andersen's story, if properly conveyed, would compensate for the inevitable flattened, two-dimensional effect of the cinema screen.[83]

'Discussing the matter … at some length' meant negotiating a large fee,[84] and credit for originating his role in the ballet. However, Massine's demonic Shoemaker is anything but flat – almost leering out of the screen as he proffers the fateful shoes to the stalls.

A married couple, Alan Carter and Joan Harris, were the assistant ballet masters. Carter and Helpmann cast 56 dancers to form the Lermontov *corps de ballet*, and Carter was in charge of the stopwatch during the filming of the ballet. Now all The Archers had to do was to fill out the rest of the cast and create a full-length

Technicolor melodrama as well as a truncated film-ballet, a form that had not yet been invented, in the space of time usually allotted to produce a far more conventional rabbit from a far more ordinary hat.

* * *

In his memoir, Powell admitted that his reaction to Junge's resignation was 'heartless'.[85] Lermontov is described that way in the film ('He has no heart, that man'), and it's clear that there are some similarities between Powell and Boris, but Pressburger resisted such a simple analogy. 'There is something of Diaghilev, something of Alex Korda, something of Michael, and quite a little bit of me.'[86] Bearing in mind that Korda reference, Lermontov evokes anthropologist Hortense Powdermaker's analysis of the supposedly powerful Hollywood studio executive's fragile confidence, writing:

One hypothesis is that executives are not completely satisfied with their roles, and, although they pretend to look down on artists and creative people, are at the same time jealous and resentful of them. ... Another possibility is that their insecurity and strong drive for power causes them to fear anyone, artist or not, who receives so much prestige that he may become a threat to the executive's power.[87]

We see this play out in Lermontov's need to control his team, and his rage against Julian, who threatens to usurp his pre-eminence in Vicky's life.

The part was also written, or redrafted, with one of their favourite actors in mind: Anton Walbrook. Powell paid tribute to how well their cast embodied the role of such strong behind-the-scenes characters: 'There was enough genius in each man or woman to enable them to appreciate the genius of the people they were playing. Fact and fiction combined to create a recognisable group of eccentric and talented individuals.'[88] Further denting the divide between on- and off-screen personnel, Pressburger himself appears as an extra at Cannes train station – a studio press release compared him to Hitchcock.

Anton Walbrook, the
most fascinating of
former matinée idols
(Photograph by
George Cannon)

Vienna-born Walbrook is superlative casting as Boris, bringing
to his portrayal of the impresario his own powerful charisma,
forged of international celebrity, continental sophistication and
potent sex appeal, of exactly the right kind. In Powell's words, it is a
performance 'filled with passion, integrity and, yes, homosexuality',[89]
as Walbrook channels the intensity of the Diaghilev–Nijinsky
romance, setting off an erotic depth charge beneath Boris's formal
interactions with Vicky's demure dancer. Watch him wring the
wooden arms of a chair while talking to Vicky about her career in a
low, breathy voice, his words and demeanour becoming increasingly
passionate. He has a way of elongating or truncating his syllables,
meticulously modulating the tempo of his words, a self-conscious
form of verbal dance.

Walbrook had been a matinée idol in 1930s German cinema under his real name Adolf Wohlbrück, adopting his signature moustache in 1933. He left Germany after the rise of the Nazi regime and in British cinema he played mysterious continentals, sometimes quite menacing characters, while keeping his sexuality secret. Like Heckroth and Pressburger, he was an exile. While he never dropped his accent during his long career in Britain, he has some of the most memorable speeches in The Archers' canon. He played Prince Albert twice, the sinister husband in the original film of *Gaslight* (Thorold Dickinson, 1940) and the 'good German' Theo in *Blimp*. He was charming and handsome, but his performances were psychologically intense, complex and brooding. Walbrook was at his best playing a seductive enigma such as the tightly wound Boris, whose defining tic is a smile that dissolves instantly into a sneer. Walbrook's performance of Boris's breakdown on stage, with his rasping announcement of Vicky's death, is almost as shocking as the gore on the railway tracks: his polished façade has cracked and fallen away.

Marius Goring, a British actor who was fluent in French and German, was also well established in The Archers' repertory troupe, having first worked with them on *The Spy in Black*. In *AMOLAD* he gives a puckish, camp performance as the celestial Conductor who craves Technicolor, but he had requested the romantic lead. As Julian in *The Red Shoes*, he almost got his wish. There is little demand here for him to play the passionate lover. His most romantic speech is written in the past tense, as if the affair were already over, and concludes with a Lermontovian compliment to his beloved: 'she was quite young, comparatively unspoiled'. Where Goring really excelled was in his imitation of a peevish, haughty conductor – an older man bursting out of his unconvincingly youthful skin.[90] Goring watched Beecham at work and turned in an impressive impersonation of a man who wielded a baton with intent and found the difference between an E flat and an E natural inherently amusing. For the first half of the film, Goring gives a comic performance: bickering with the balletomanes, swept away in a stage boat as he makes fruitless

Marius Goring gives a note-perfect impersonation of a haughty conductor
(Photograph by Alistair Phillips)

enquiries backstage. As he attempts to command the orchestra for
the first time, a comically timed honk of brass and a wall of stony
faces turn the joke on him. Goring plays to his comic strengths and
situates Julian's story in second place behind Vicky's – she's always
deadly serious.

One would love to think that French Ludmilla Tchérina, who
plays the outgoing ballerina Irina Boronskaja, was cast because of
her impressive dance credentials (she made her début at the Ballets
Russes de Monte-Carlo). In fact, Powell had spotted her and become
besotted with her in her first film, *Un revenant* (Christian-Jaque,
1946): 'sluttish and lovely, twenty years old, a face to dream about,
skin like the petal of a rose, eyes like twin moons'.[91] The fact that she
could dance was a bonus for Powell, but the fact that she didn't speak
English was irrelevant. She is sweetness itself in the film, very funny

Robert Helpmann, Esmond Knight, Ludmilla Tchérina, Albert Bassermann and
Léonide Massine (Photograph by Alistair Phillips)

and then suddenly poignant when Boris rejects her. A vivid screen
presence, she would appear in two more Archers' productions.

More Powell and Pressburger regulars returned. Esmond
Knight, his eyesight still badly damaged from his wartime service,
played Livy. Jerry Verno, a veteran of Powell's Quota Quickie days,
gives an appealing comic turn as the Cockney stage-door keeper. Eric
Berry, who had appeared in Powell's 1937 *The Edge of the World*,
plays Boris's assistant Dimitri. Comic favourite Hay Petrie plays the
lawyer – and it was to be his final role, as he died aged just 53, the
summer before the film was released.

The Red Shoes saw the final appearance of another great actor,
Albert Bassermann, who plays Boris's peacemaker-designer Sergei.
Bassermann was German, an acclaimed actor of stage and cinema,

whose career included a handful of great Expressionist films. When he left Germany with his Jewish wife in the 1930s (just as Heckroth did), he spoke no English. He still didn't by the time he appeared in English-language films such as Hitchcock's *Foreign Correspondent* (1940) and *The Red Shoes*. He learned his lines phonetically, but delivered them in an appealingly rich, barrelling tone, and with a mischievous touch of humour. Unfortunately, Bassermann did not have a pleasant experience on set, with Powell directing his temper at the actor and his wife. Walbrook was so outraged at this treatment of such a great man that he threatened never to work with The Archers again – a promise he made good on, until 1955's *Oh … Rosalinda!!*

The Bassermann business was a bitter incident in the history of the film, but nobody would have such strong words to say against the film, or prove so difficult to cast, as Moira Shearer, the young Sadler's Wells dancer whom The Archers chose to play Vicky Page.

Cast and crew of *The Red Shoes*, on the set of the ballet (Photograph by George Cannon)

5 Balletomania: 'To live? To dance'

The opening shot of the film, soundtracked by a roar of protest.
A steep staircase seemingly out of a German Expressionist film:
a grubby window throws distorted squares of light on to the wall.
It's a Dickensian scene. Inside a gaslight burns; outside a black
streetlamp. A man in evening dress descends the stairs and checks his
fob watch. The guards can no longer hold the doors shut, the students
are forcing their way in. 'Down with tyrants,' cries one off-screen.
With trepidation, the guards release the mob.

* * *

The students who tear into the Royal Opera House at the start of
the film represent the arrival of a new season in British ballet. In
1946, *Good Housekeeping* informed its readers that: 'Ballet-going,
since the war, has become one of this nation's new habits, like (and
generally involving) queuing, or Spam.'[92] That was the year that the
Sadler's Wells Ballet Company inaugurated its new residency in the
reopened Royal Opera House, with a performance of *The Sleeping
Beauty*. Postwar austerity bit deep: clothing coupons for costumes
and camouflage paint for set-dressing.

Ballets Russes alumna Ninette de Valois had founded Sadler's
Wells, later the Royal Ballet, as the Vic-Wells Ballet in 1931. It was
the fruit of her professional collaboration, since 1926, with theatre
manager Lilian Baylis, whose life's mission was to bring high culture
to the working classes. De Valois was born Edris Stannus in County
Wicklow in 1898, and this Irishwoman with a French stage name and
Russian training was a central figure in the development of Britain's
national ballet culture. 'I wanted a tradition,' she wrote in 1963, 'and
I set out to establish one.'[93] She was also instrumental in enabling
Moira Shearer to appear in *The Red Shoes*.

Dame Ninette de Valois, photographed in 1960 (Ben Martin/ Getty Images)

In the 1910s and 1920s the Russian influence, primarily via Diaghilev and his company, including choreographer Michel Fokine, nudged British ballet away from music-hall entertainment and closer to high art, and to a respectable career for middle-class British girls. Anna Pavlova inspired many young well-heeled girls to become ballet dancers, including de Valois who first danced in Britain, and Alicia Markova (born Lilian Marks in London), who both later joined the Ballets Russes. In 1924 Anton Dolin (Patrick Healey-Kaye from West Sussex – who was the first male dancer to perform *en pointe*, in 1924) became the company's principal *danseur*, and in 1925, Diaghilev commissioned London-born composer Constant Lambert to write a score for *Roméo et Juliette*. In the 1930s, following Diaghilev's death, there were multiple efforts to create a British ballet, including the formation of the Vic-Wells (with Lambert – and Markova and Dolin as guest artists), and Marie Rambert's company, which also features in *The Red Shoes*, when Vicky performs at the Mercury in Notting Hill with Rambert herself in the audience. In 1932, British film *Dance, Pretty Lady* featured Rambert's dancers and choreography by Frederick Ashton alongside its melodramatic story. Ashton would create some of the best British ballets, beginning with *Façade* in 1931. Also in 1931 de Valois choreographed *Job: A Masque for Dancing*, with music by Ralph Vaughan Williams – known as the first British-made ballet. Economist John Maynard Keynes, husband to Lydia Lopokova, offered his support and cultural cachet to de Valois's company, giving ballet another nudge up the social order.

'Balletomane', a loanword from Russian, appeared in the 1930s and referred to the kind of excitable devotee played for laughs in the film's opening scene.[94] Ballet's popularity in Britain could be measured by the tickets sold, but also by the runaway success of Noel Streatfeild's 1936 children's book *Ballet Shoes*, an old-fashioned story about three adopted sisters attending a London stage school headed by retired Russian prima ballerina Madame Fidolia. As *The Red Shoes* would do in the 1940s, *Ballet Shoes* inspired girls to clamour for ballet lessons – a request granted by the growing number of ballet schools in the country. In the story it is the youngest sister, redheaded Posy Fossil, who has the real genius for ballet, and aspires to study with eminent Czech dancer Monsieur Manoff, a Diaghilev alumnus who promises to make her into a 'beautiful artiste'. Posy is single-minded in pursuit of her goal, confident in her talent and sure of what she needs to succeed. This results in some atrociously selfish behaviour, and she is rebuked by her guardians: 'It was all very well to be ambitious, but ambition should not kill the nice qualities in you.'[95] Shearer, 10 years old and studying ballet with a friend of the author, appeared as Posy in advertisements, a juvenile rehearsal for playing Vicky.

In 1939, thanks to the efforts of de Valois, Rambert and their cohort, Arnold Haskell could say: 'To-day, for the first time in the history of the art, ballet is indigenous in England.'[96] That year, the Vic-Wells presented a triumphant *Sleeping Beauty* at a gala in Covent Garden with Margot Fonteyn (Margaret Hookham from Reigate) dancing the lead. She was the company's new ballerina, replacing Markova. Wartime altered the course of the ballet wave but did not halt it. While the Royal Opera House became a dance hall, Sadler's Wells toured the nation, on an exhausting schedule that took in factories and army bases. By the end of the war, ballet audiences were bigger and more diverse than before, though hardly as vast as the audience for cinema. The Royal Opera House reopened with lower ticket prices and some noted with distaste how many of the audience arrived in day wear. Many doubtless brought (Spam) sandwiches too, like Julian's friend Ike (Gordon Littmann), up in the cheap seats where casual dress is the order of the day, and there is no room for his neighbour to spread out her cloak.

The ballets were different too. Minimalism and restraint were prized above spectacle and high emotion. De Valois staged realist ballets such as 1944's *Miracle in the Gorbals* (choreographed by Helpmann, who joined Vic-Wells in 1933), which is the production in which Powell first saw Shearer dance, following a tip from Stewart Granger. *The Red Shoes* originally featured a ballet of this ilk in the opening scene, named *Caledonian Market*. However, it was replaced by *Heart of Fire* (a likely nod to *The Firebird*, premiered by Diaghilev's Ballets Russes in 1910), danced in front of classical ruins (surely a reference to its own modernity) and costumes that incorporate streaks of paint on the dancers' tights, foreshadowing Vicky's death.

Shearer had begun her professional career during the war, so she had witnessed this growing democratisation of ballet in person. She was born in Scotland in 1926, as Moira Shearer King, but spent her early years in Rhodesia, in modern-day Zimbabwe, where she started ballet classes at the age of six, which she continued after her family moved to London. She was taken to Covent Garden when

The Ballet Lermontov presents *Heart of Fire*

she was eight, where she saw Massine dance and became besotted with the Russian ballet, which is the style in which she was trained. Later, Shearer danced five different roles that renowned Russian ballerina Tamara Karsavina had originated at the Ballets Russes, and consulted her before dancing *Giselle* at Sadler's Wells. In 1941, she joined Mona Inglesby's new company, International Ballet, in London, before moving to Sadler's Wells in 1942. De Valois nicknamed this fierce young dancer 'Little King', though she never became one of her favourites. Joining this more illustrious company meant re-entering the *corps de ballet* (as Vicky Page does when she joins the Ballet Lermontov). However, Shearer was given some solo parts almost immediately; by 1946 she was originating a role in Ashton's *Symphonic Variations*. Although she received excellent reviews, she often bristled against the regime at Sadler's Wells, which this sensitive young woman found oppressive. Shearer said that de Valois's determination to create

Moira Shearer,
Sadler's Wells's
soloist and film star

an English ballerina out of Fonteyn frustrated her in her career, and
the development of her dancing: 'there can only be one talent and
everybody else somehow must be subservient and not try to do well'.[97]

Fear of losing her position at the company was one of the
reasons why, for several months, Shearer refused the role of Vicky
Page. The mere idea of leaving to do a film, let alone becoming a
film star, would challenge the company's hierarchy and she worried
she would be punished for drawing attention to herself. Two things
changed her mind. One was the reassuring presence of Massine and
Helpmann. Massine had returned to Britain after spending the war
touring America with the Ballets Russes de Monte-Carlo. The second
was a Lermontovian command from de Valois, who called her into the

office and said: 'For heaven's sake, child, get this off your chest *and* ours, because I can't stand these men bothering all of us any longer.'[98] Shearer's first 24 hours in Nice were a hot-and-cold immersion into film-making. Fresh off the plane from London, she was treated to a gift (a pair of red sandals) and a steak lunch, then fitted for her character's Paris wardrobe. Early the next morning, she was asked to perform the final scene, her character's leap to her death – a task made more gruelling by the intense heat and a panic over a lost tutu.

After the film was released, Shearer became a reluctant celebrity, especially in the US, where she was compared to Ginger Rogers. Shearer had long been renowned for her beauty and her red hair was radiant in Technicolor; Americans who flocked to see Sadler's Wells on tour were reportedly disappointed if they saw Fonteyn instead. By starring in *The Red Shoes*, Shearer may have eclipsed Fonteyn in the wider world, but within ballet there was lingering disdain for cinema. De Valois made it clear that 'most people in highbrow artistic circles considered a film contract to be little better than a pact with the devil'.[99] However, in 1948, when Fonteyn was indisposed, de Valois allowed Ashton to choose Shearer to dance the lead in his *Cinderella*, the first English three-act ballet. Shearer recalls her triumph in the role, not as a story of overnight success à la Vicky taking over from Irina, but as an episode that alienated her from her peers.

Shearer remained embarrassed about *The Red Shoes* for the rest of her life. Powell was happy to cast a dancer on the verge of greatness, but Shearer was a perfectionist, and mortified that the film captured a performance containing what she considered flaws, such as her 'spiky' hand movements. Shearer believed that the film caught her on the brink of 'a big jump forward, technically, artistically, in every way'.[100] She was much happier with her dancing in *The Tales of Hoffmann*, choreographed by Ashton, four years later. The snippets in *The Red Shoes* from the company's repertoire, such as the scene of her dancing *Coppélia* (a ballet she did not like) demonstrate her range and skill, although the camera angles do not give a complete view of her technique. Shearer's strengths as a dancer were technical brilliance as well as speed, lightness and her jumps. The impish bounce of 'The Dance of the Red Shoes' suits her style, but few of the steps in the central ballet challenged her or gave her the opportunity to add her own expressiveness. Helpmann himself called his choreography 'undistinguished';[101] Arlene Croce called it 'thin to the point of misty suggestion'.[102] There are not very many steps, and the edits are so fast as to obliterate many of them. The trick camerawork overrode Shearer's natural ability in speed and height. Both in the rushes and in the final film, all she could see were her own self-perceived failings: 'There it was, sort of pickled in time and on film and there was no opportunity to perfect and improve it. It was a very depressing experience,' she told Dale Harris. 'Most people absolutely love it. I just felt that they didn't know how it could have been.'[103] When she later worked with the modernist Russian choreographer George Balanchine, he paid her the highest compliment in rehearsal, telling her he had no idea that she could dance so well, because he had seen *The Red Shoes*.

Shearer shared the low opinion of the film from elsewhere in the ballet world too. Many ballet folk took exception to Cardiff's 'dishonest' camera, the camera tricks and edits that adulterated the representation of the dancer's steps. The filming process had not been orthodox either. The dancers were not able to perform the ballet straight through but had to repeat short chains of steps a few seconds long. It was a very unnatural way to work, especially for classically trained dancers. At Covent Garden no one would tell Fonteyn to take her entrance again because the lights weren't completely set right, but at Pinewood that was exactly what was expected of Shearer and Helpmann. Then there were the physical discomforts: the heat of the megawatt lights and the floor, which was concrete under the boards and very punishing on the feet.

There was another timing issue that tarnished the film. *The Red Shoes*, arriving between the grand reopening of the Royal Opera House in 1946 and Sadler's Wells's first US tour in 1949, was out of step with British ballet culture's self-image. It was emotional, spectacular, aristocratic and very Russian. Even after her years at

Sadler's Wells, critics detected the Russian style in Shearer's dancing, for example, let alone the Russian accents and names of many of the characters. Some objected to how the film presents backstage life as teeming with tantrums and high drama, although Helpmann insisted that in relation to the real thing, 'it was quite understated'.[104] The Lermontov company also lived a life of luxury far removed from the experience of a working dancer in the 1940s. One critic took exception to the film's scenes of 'ballerinas stepping out of Rolls-Royces in Floral Street' in comparison to the lived reality of 'the reek of sweat in the classroom, the mouldiness of a landlady's breakfast in Scunthorpe'.[105] The film also featured a deeply male-dominated company and women forced to choose between marriage and career: de Valois, who led her company with fierce discipline, and was married herself, might scoff that it all belonged to a lost era.

There was a gulf, however, between image and reality. Russian influence, and Russian competition, were not that distant from British ballet. De Valois's professionalism was a legacy of her time under the far more ruthless Diaghilev. She hired men in key creative roles and

Ballet deluxe: Vicky in evening dress at Boris's villa

spoke of women as ballet's 'housekeepers'. Very few female dancers were married, let alone mothers. When she married Arthur Connell, a doctor, in 1935, she initially kept it secret from her colleagues. When Shearer married Ludovic Kennedy in 1950, her peers were shocked, partly because the journalist had no connection to the ballet, partly because ballerinas didn't marry: 'All the eyebrows went flying high,' recalled dancer Nadia Nerina.[106] Shearer retired from dancing shortly after she had her first child in 1952, though she had tried valiantly to continue. She worked instead as an actress, on stage and in film, and she had three more children. *The Red Shoes* poked a finger in an open wound.

Pressburger's first screenplay had been set once upon a very different time, 'at a period when relief over the outcome of the First World War has not become over-shadowed by the prospects of a Second'.[107] This timestamp disappeared from the script before shooting, possibly after Powell instructed Heckroth to design the ballet in modern dress. If there were any doubt over the fashions, the newspaper that Vicky catches on the terrace at midnight is filled with the news of 1947. By the time they wrote the novelisation in 1977, Powell added a note to Pressburger's first draft, 'Early thirties [*sic*] better than 20's [*sic*]', but the novel begins: 'Upon a spring evening in London in the twenties of this twentieth century of ours, the Ballets [*sic*] Lermontov was at long last at Covent Garden Opera House.'[108] In that opening paragraph there is a well-placed jibe about exotic stage names, 'that well-known dancer Hilda Boot became Tamara Butsova overnight'.[109] For the denizens of Covent Garden, the most (only?) up-to-date facet of *The Red Shoes* film was Victoria Page's Anglophone name writ large on the Ballet Lermontov bills. Even that had a precedent: Bristol-born Phyllis Bedells danced successfully under her own name from the 1910s to the 1930s, becoming the first prima ballerina of London's Empire Theatre of Varieties in 1914.

If the film is a little out-of-time, it was not for want of trying to fit in. *The Red Shoes* uses many strategies to situate itself into contemporary ballet culture. First there is the presence of ballet

Ballet realism:
the *barre* class
(Photograph by
George Cannon)

luminaries, including Rambert, Helpmann and Massine, plus Shearer
and the carefully assembled *corps*, many of whom were dancing
sections from ballets they made famous. Massine's name appears next
to his Andersen-esque ballet *La Boutique fantasque* on a poster; all
the ballets listed on the posters are real and have a place in British
ballet history, apart from *Heart of Fire* and *The Red Shoes*. Vicky's
tragedy encompasses the stories of Nijinsky, Pavlova and Duncan,
but also the story of English ballerina Diana Gould, who had been
invited to join the Ballets Russes by Diaghilev and then Pavlova, but
both died before she could accept. Pavlova famously called Gould the
only English dancer who 'had a soul', and she was a leading dancer
in the 1930s, before retiring after her marriage to violinist Yehudi
Menuhin. After the triumph of *The Red Shoes*, Boris sets his team to
work on *La Belle meunière*, which is a deep in-joke for either balletic
or cinematic circles. It is the name of a character in Massine's 1919
ballet *Le Tricorne*, the Miller's Wife and therefore also a tip of the
three-cornered hat to *A Canterbury Tale*. It may also be a dig at
J. Arthur Rank, whose family made their fortune in flour. A draft of
the screenplay refers to *La Belle meunière* by Marcel Pagnol – and
the French writer-director indeed released a film of that title in 1948,
although the reference was dropped from the film.

The Red Shoes is not shooting for realism, so these references are more to do with fantasy world-building than believability. As Adrienne L. McLean writes, in her comprehensive study of what does and does not make balletic sense in the film: 'we really learn more about what the film's creators think about ballet than we do about what its performers feel about it'.[110] Just as the music lovers and the balletomanes are at odds as to whether Heart of Fire is a performance for the ears, or a spectacle for the eyes, the experience of The Red Shoes differs for cinephiles and ballet lovers. Nevertheless, The Red Shoes retains a pre-eminent position within the history of the ballet film. For Croce, 'there really is no other ballet film',[111] and its success in influencing young people to take barre classes surpasses even that of Ballet Shoes. This was most notably celebrated in the 1975 musical A Chorus Line, the book for which was drawn from interviews with Broadway 'Gypsies', many of whom enthused about the film, but anecdotal examples abound.

It is too simple, as we have seen, to say The Red Shoes's position in the field is simply due to its achievement of aesthetic excellence in both cinema and ballet. Opinions are divided, and a ballet film is no novelty. Dance has been integral to film since the days of Loïe Fuller's hypnotic Serpentine Dances, and artistes from Pavlova (The Dumb Girl of Portici, Lois Weber and Phillips Smalley, 1916) to Fonteyn (The Little Ballerina, Lewis Gilbert, 1947) had appeared in films before Shearer. The Red Shoes distinguishes itself from many predecessors in a few aspects. It focuses on a young woman's story, but portrays ballerinas as devotees of art, rather than immature women distracted by rivalry and obsession (as in dance-school films such as La Mort du cygne (Jean Benoît-Lévy and Marie Epstein, 1937), remade in English as The Unfinished Dance (Henry Koster, 1947)). Despite lapses in its earlier drafts, it removes ballet from the music hall and considerations of class or sexual impropriety as in the adaptations of Compton Mackenzie's novel Carnival or of Robert E. Sherwood's play Waterloo Bridge. Although it is a far-fetched take on the Diaghilev–Nijinsky dynamic, it is not as grotesque or lecherous as

The rehearsal studio in Paris is a temple to art

1931 pre-Code film *The Mad Genius* (Michael Curtiz), whose story originates in a carnival sideshow milieu (based on a 1929 play, and not on Romola Nijinsky's memoir).

This sombre contemplation of ballet as a religion creates one of Powell and Pressburger's finest nests for magic. Andrew Moor writes that for Powell and Pressburger, '"Art" itself is a symbolic territory … full of strange spectacles.'[112] *The Red Shoes*'s concern with art for art's sake removes its players from the realm of realism, to a sun-blessed coast where genius thrives and where the act of dancing on one's toes is seen not as the result of arduous, painful practice, but as an astonishing miracle. A marvel in red satin. While other ballet films, such as Ben Hecht's *Specter of the Rose* (1946), portrayed high-strung performers fixated on the tragic roles they played in the classic ballets, *The Red Shoes* dissolves the barrier between dancer and dance almost entirely – especially in the rich symbolism of the centrepiece ballet. *The Red Shoes* operates on a level deeper than drama and raises more malign demons than the well-worn topics of career-romance conflicts, the Svengali complex and the eccentricity of a brilliant mind. *The Red Shoes* fulfils the promise of its fairy-tale origin to become its own, enduring legend.

6 The Ballet: 'I am that horror'

Alone in a dark, deserted part of the city, separated from her boyfriend, The Girl dances into the path of monsters: hunched, half-dead ghouls with half-hidden faces. They circle her, coming closer, until she is surrounded. A spotlight falls on her and she begins to lead the monsters in a dance. They mimic her turns, her steps; she points to the sky, and they leap upwards. The monsters come closer, forming a dais that holds The Girl aloft, in the spotlight, posing *arabesque*.

* * *

Contemporary viewers of *The Red Shoes* tend to agree with the film's first critics on one point. The extended ballet sequence is far and away the highlight of the film: astonishing both in its artistry and its audacity. In the *Sunday Times*, Dilys Powell called it an 'extreme pleasure', commenting that the writer and director were unrivalled in 'this matter of enjoyed authority and daring'.[113] The *Observer*'s C. A. Lejeune praised Heckroth in particular, saying 'the wedding of movement and colour here is almost perfect'.[114] Michael Powell was justifiably proud of his centrepiece. He told Irish writer Monk Gibbon, in a monograph commissioned to accompany the film:

For me the ballet of *The Red Shoes* is a gathering together of my whole accumulated knowledge of the film medium – disciplined by music, enhanced by colour, with the very maximum of physical action – which films should transfer better than anything – and at the same time a distillation of story-telling. It is a gathering together of all we've learnt. My memory goes back to the very first films. My ambition goes far ahead of today.[115]

Much can be drawn out of Powell's poetic description. Evidently, the ballet is a *Gesamtkunstwerk* of art, dance, cinematography and

'Extreme pleasure': Shearer and Helpmann in the ballet sequence

narrative. It is also a 'composed film' – closer to animation than live action, betraying the influence of *Fantasia* – in which music has the 'authority'. The dominance of music is a theme that runs through the film, with various members of the company telling Vicky that nothing else matters. Each scene originated as a Heckroth painting, which the rest of the crew recreated in live action, perfectly in time to the music track. Powell considered the sequence an homage to silent technique, due to the substitution splices, varied camera speeds and visual storytelling. Massine's shoemaker prances in front of painted backdrops like the dancing devils in trick films by Georges Méliès or Segundo de Chomón. It has connections he doesn't quite elucidate to the contemporary Hollywood musical. It is also very clearly infused with the imagery and tone of horror cinema. This sequence would prove deeply influential to both the latter genres, supporting Powell's claim that the sequence is ahead of its time.

First, let's look backwards. The appearance of 'dream ballet' in musical theatre, which transferred into Hollywood adaptations, was a natural development from the presence of dream sequences and visions in narrative 'ballet d'action'. On Broadway in 1943, Agnes de Mille[116] choreographed a 15-minute dream ballet for Rodgers and Hammerstein's *Oklahoma!* stage show and musical films soon followed suit. Hollywood scholar Lisa Duffy defines the dream ballet as: 'an extended dance sequence which takes place in the mind of a character, revealing their own unconscious thoughts, fears and desires through the medium of dance'.[117] She describes the arc of the classic dream ballet as beginning with *Oklahoma!* on stage and ending with the film adaptation in 1955. *The Red Shoes* sits near the midpoint of this period, though it is differentiated by its Anglo-European and Russian style of dance and expression. Nevertheless, it was pivotal. Gene Kelly harnessed the success of the film to persuade MGM executives to allow him to include a 17-minute 'dream ballet' in *An American in Paris* (Vincente Minnelli, 1951).

We can situate *The Red Shoes* ballet in a tradition of film dance that also incorporates the 'opened-out' impossible staging of the climactic performance in a backstage musical, such as the Busby Berkeley choreographed sequences in *Gold Diggers of 1933* (Mervyn LeRoy, 1933). However, the ballet appears halfway through the film, wrongfooting the expectations of viewers accustomed to that structure. It is also important to emphasise that *The Red Shoes*'s ballet aspires to something other than the professional, uplifting and communal entertainment value that Richard Dyer defines as the motivation of the classic Hollywood musical. Instead, it aspires to the status of high art, is emotionally harrowing and decidedly individualistic. As The Archers' manifesto puts it: 'No artist believes in escapism.' It also owes something to extended ballet sequences in films such as the nearly seven-minute *Swan Lake* performance choreographed by George Balanchine in *I Was an Adventuress* (Gregory Ratoff, 1940), starring Norwegian ex-ballerina Vera Zorina, or the four-minute *Swan Lake* in *The Unfinished Dance*.

Cinema audiences were familiar with a ballet interlude, although *The Red Shoes* breaks with the convention of shooting ballet in an elevated long shot that takes in the entire stage to show both the formation of the dancers and their footwork. Powell spares no reverence for the theatrical experience, using cinematic grammar, including close-ups and visual effects, throughout. This is a cinematic space, not a stage. Powell insisted that there would be no shots of the audience, as the cinema spectators were to imagine that they were in the theatre themselves, but we are also reminded that Vicky plans to imagine a wall between herself and the audience when dancing. In a film, the spectator's privileged position is that of spying on the action, rather than accepting the invitation offered by the theatre's proscenium arch. When Vicky dances through the carnival, the coloured squares of cellophane that fall around her represent both the gels from the stage footlights, and those on the studio cameras. Or, perhaps, the small cellophane window that Grischa peeks through

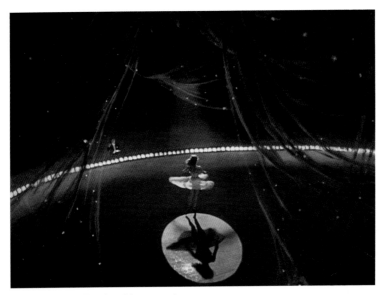

A film ballet that breaks with convention

on the opening night of *Heart of Fire*, which offers performers backstage a sparkling, hazily distorted view of the audience. Soothing her stage-fright, Boris assures her that she is 'not dancing for an audience', but only for the other members of the company.

One departure in *The Red Shoes* is nesting the dream ballet within the performance that is the output of the backstage toil depicted within the film. There is just one break in the continued illusion of the ballet, when the audience(s) both in the cinema and the Opéra de Monte-Carlo are expected to applaud. Perversely, this breathing space is provided by Vicky dashing offstage for a costume change and to dab the sweat from her brow. There are no other such concessions to realism. This transition prompts Vicky's awakening from the dream ballet back to the ballet proper. Earlier, a close-up of her sweating, painted, shocked face began the dream-ballet sequence, and encapsulated what it will reveal: the horror disguised within the grace and beauty of the dancer on stage.

Vicky takes fright on stage, and the dream ballet begins

Each droplet of sweat on Vicky's forehead carries a double meaning. It represents her labour, the effort and the corporeality obscured by the dancer's grace. It is also a signifier of anxiety and mental derangement. Consider the close-up of Sister Ruth towards the end of *Black Narcissus*: red lips and a dewy brow convey her disordered state in contrast to the calm, unadorned serenity of the convent she has left behind. It was Cardiff who first pointed out to Powell that a ballerina's face in close-up looks more demonic than beautiful, and suggested the dancers wear different make-up for close and long shots. 'Anyone seeing faces backstage might recoil in terror or revulsion,' he wrote in his memoir. 'Close up, it was as grotesque as a Fauvist painting but from the auditorium it looked quite natural.'[118] However, in certain places, Powell chooses to linger on this greasepaint mask. A direction in the screenplay that didn't make it into the film underlines the point. 'CAMERA TRACKS BACK further and further. VICKY wears heavy ballet make-up like all of them and as she gets further and further away, she appears more and more beautiful.' We see Vicky close-up in her stage make-up at key points in the film, such as when she hears Boris talking about 'the doubtful comforts of human love' backstage at *Giselle*, and during the final confrontation in her dressing room, as she weeps. The impression of simplicity is created by a 'great agony of body and spirit' and Vicky gives her sweat, her tears and finally her blood for her art.

Briefly, let's resist the temptation to follow The Girl/Vicky through the ballet, as the compositions often shrink her down to a corner or a low sector of the frame, anyway. The recreations of Heckroth's paintings dominate the view. Heckroth felt such ownership of the sequence that he confided in his diary that he felt he should really be the director of the film – a position he reversed after seeing Powell in action. The sequence is short for a ballet, but it is a long time to spend looking at art and abstractions in a commercial film in 1948. In *Spellbound* (1945), Alfred Hitchcock collaborated with Salvador Dalí to create a dream sequence of about 20 minutes, mostly directed by designer-turned-director William Cameron

Menzies, but producer David O. Selznick insisted that it be trimmed to under three minutes for release. This too contains cutaways to the 'audience' or rather the treatment room in which Gregory Peck's character is narrating this dream to his doctors.

The duration is vital. The sequence is often compared to The Archers' feature-length forays into 'composed film' in *The Tales of Hoffmann* and *Oh … Rosalinda!!*. It is also a partner to the 17-minute scene in their next film, *The Small Back Room* (1949), in which David Farrar's Sammy defuses a booby-trapped bomb on Chesil Beach in real time. This sequence is likewise a test of the lead character's skill – will Sammy defuse the bomb? Can Vicky dance the lead role? – and an insight into their mental fragility. Sammy is working sober after a drinking binge; his sweat falls into his eyes and distorts his vision. Powell acknowledged in both films the influence of German Expressionism: the painted backdrops, deep shadows, camera distortions and tilted angles are employed both to convey the mental disturbance of the film's protagonist, but also to create an avowedly artistic style of cinema. Any sequence of this extended length is a demonstration, almost a boast, of film-making virtuosity, one that incorporates a range of artforms, and artists, all striving to exceed expectations. Powell didn't just expect the audience to endure the ballet, but to applaud it. As Andrew Moor points out, the film deflects as much as its dazzles; it presents the ballet as a product of the company's labour, but also as an impossible spectacle that could only be conjured by 'the secret, mesmeric trickery of which cinema alone is capable'.[119]

The ballet promises to show the company's production of *The Red Shoes* (with the action running left to right) but after that sweaty close-up, it segues into a different story altogether, revealing the secrets of Vicky's subconscious (roughly right to left), a transition into her inner life pre-empted by those subjective whip pans in the Mercury Theatre. First, in the fairy-tale section, The Girl expresses her desire for the shoes, or rather the vision she sees in the shop window (this double exposure is just the first of the cinematic tricks

Heckroth's painting of The Girl seeing herself in the red shoes

in the sequence), of herself, dancing beautifully *en pointe* in a tutu. Here the personas of Vicky and The Girl merge – both aspire to be a ballerina. The Shoemaker causes night to fall and The Girl goes out dancing at the carnival, to jazzy strains of music. She dances gleefully at first through a sleazy sideshow (which echoes the exemplar film of German Expressionism, *The Cabinet of Dr. Caligari* (Robert Wiene, 1920)), where she is partnered by a succession of men, from different social classes. Then her boyfriend is kidnapped, and when his cellophane portrait floats down to the floor she dances right across it (all that is shown are her scarlet feet). She grows weary of dancing and attempts to go home to her grandmother, but she cannot enter the house, lit by a dubiously inviting firelight glow – the shadow of The Shoemaker extends across the stage, representing the power that he exerts over her. She has chosen dance over the security of home and betrothal, and this prompts a crisis.

The second, psychic horror half of the ballet begins with that close-up of Vicky's sweaty face as she fully takes over the character of The Girl. Her sickened expression is explained by fast cuts in which the demonic Shoemaker is replaced by both Julian and Boris in her imagination, foreshadowing her choice between marriage and career. The pose they adopt, arms aloft, is repeated by Boris after his 'triumph' in the dressing-room scene. She falls from a mountainous land into an abstract space where the newspaper that caught her eye on the terrace transforms into a man (Helpmann) with whom she dances, representing her uneasy relationship with the sudden fame that is about to envelop her, the destiny that Boris has determined for her.

The official synopsis for the ballet gives a guided tour of the mental locations that Vicky travels through, e.g. The Dead City of Failure. As Adrienne L. McLean points out, it is unlikely that the audience will follow this precise psychic geography, but the effect of the ballet is to overwhelm with spectacle and emotion, to

Vicky toys with the idea of fame

excavate a deeper horror prompted by the fairy-tale inspiration, the consequences of pride and ambition, and to pre-empt the action in the second half of the film. There is no need to stress the similarities between Boris and the Satanic-tempter Shoemaker or Julian and The Boy, although his transfiguration into The Priest is intriguing. Massine as The Shoemaker leans into the frame for close-ups and moves at a frenetic pace – his wild hair and heavy make-up are distracting at all times. By contrast Helpmann, in his several roles, is subdued, almost anonymous. One exception is the newspaper dance, in which he leaps and turns, but his eyes are always clearly focused on Vicky as he dances around her – he is a figment of her imagination. Contrast that with Massine's *jetée* entrance a moment after he disappears – he redefines the space around Vicky, motivates a change in lighting and backdrop and spins her into another location. We might say that the ballet sequence doesn't represent Vicky's dilemma between Boris/dance and Julian/marriage as much as explore how she feels about the decision she has already made – she needs to dance as she needs to live, and she wants to dance for Boris.

Unlike the sunny village square setting that opens the ballet, and far from her own upper-class milieu, the land of Vicky's nightmares veers between hostile nature, and a seedy, criminalised urban space. However, even in the dream ballet, Shearer dances lightly, delicately. Her weightless movements (emphasised by Cardiff's speed-tricks), along with her white, tight-waisted dress and her blue hair ribbon, emphasise her youth. She is a child among adults and in adult spaces, poised on the verge of womanhood, of artistic greatness. Twirling her around, The Shoemaker delivers her to a spooky red-light district. Vicky's trepidation in this sexualised, urban space, so far removed from the cosseted world of ballet, could suggest her fear of sex, of life outside marriage, or possibly of a return to the status of a music-hall dancer. After passing through a high wall, she encounters monsters as The Shoemaker shows her a vision in a reflecting pool.

Vicky mimics The Shoemaker's gesture of splaying his hands in front of her face and the demons lift her into the spotlight and

A seedy, criminalised urban space; The Shoemaker shows Vicky a vision – of her future?

from there to the ballroom sequence that we know Boris has deleted from the ballet, and therefore exists only in Vicky's mind. She dances down to the footlights and sees Julian conducting in front of her before she dances with a princely lover from classical ballet. She then performs a group dance with two other couples. This is a venue for imagination and artistic freedom – this is where, as Julian promised, Vicky transforms into a bird, a flower, a cloud, with no sense of the effort required to 'leave the ground in the first place'. It is also a dangerous place: ballroom dancing and classical ballet involve what scholar Katharina Lindner calls 'the performative reconstitution

The Girl dances into danger (Photograph by Baron)

of heteronormativity',[120] with men representing strength, leading and lifting a partner, while the women follow, embodying grace and softness. Suddenly self-consciousness returns: she is dancing for Boris, who watches from his box in the theatre while waves crash against the stage. This is where the dream ballet ends. Vicky dashes offstage for the applause-break and reappears as The Girl in rags, helplessly watching her grandmother's funeral procession, but unable to enter the church. She takes The Shoemaker's knife to cut off her feet but it transforms into a branch and she dances with him instead in a wild frenzy, the screen bathed in a red glow. The Priest saves her, removes the shoes, and she dies in his arms. The Shoemaker takes the shoes back to his shop and proffers them to the audience.

Peril is afoot. The Girl yearns to be the dancer in the red shoes and she suffers and dies for these sins of pride and ambition. Vicky's trajectory is more complex: her demons transport her to her artistic apotheosis. The monstrous portion of the dream ballet is

The Girl dies in the arms of The Priest

terrifying, and appears entirely incongruous, set alongside the film's elegant interiors and postcard views of the Côte d'Azur. Yet horror is fundamental to *The Red Shoes*. The violence of Andersen's tale finds its fullest expression in Vicky's death on the tracks, but is also evoked by the nightmare ballet, and hinted at throughout the film. Listen out for how many times the word 'horror' itself is mentioned, including Vicky's prophetic admission to Boris at their first meeting that 'I am that horror'. Although The Archers are not making a film about the war for once, the atrocities of the conflict and the camps would have been a fresh memory for both the film's pan-European cast and crew, many of whom are exiled from their home countries, and the similarly international staff of the Ballet Lermontov. Powell and Pressburger's morbid streak is their own, though, and often explicitly connected to female bodies: from the glue assaults of *A Canterbury Tale* to the psychosexual derangement of the sisters in *Black Narcissus*.

It is now difficult to imagine the subgenre of ballet horror typified by Dario Argento's *Suspiria* (1977) and Darren Aronofsky's *Black Swan* (2010) without Powell and Pressburger's gory precedent. Close-ups of blistered, bleeding feet are a staple of ballet films even outside that genre, such as *The Turning Point* (Herbert Ross, 1977). However, in the 1940s, critics recoiled at this gruesome inclination. Horror was not predominant in British cinema at this point – the heyday of Hammer Horror was years away – but ballet has always been ghoulish. Even Henry Koster's much sweeter Hollywood ballet drama *The Unfinished Dance* features a dancing demon and a scary sequence in which child actress Margaret O'Brien runs through a dark theatre. Ballets in the classical and modern repertoires deal tragic, often bloody violence to their female leads; in most versions of *Swan Lake*, both lovers drown, Giselle dies at the end of Act I and reappears as a ghost for Act II. Anna Pavlova premiered *The Dying Swan* in 1907, and famously requested the costume on her deathbed in 1931. It inspired a silent film of 1917, about a ballerina strangled by an artist obsessed with death.[121] Heroines are often cursed or

enchanted, as in *Swan Lake*, or *The Sleeping Beauty*. Doppelgängers
abound, along with elements of the uncanny, even in lighter fare
such as *The Nutcracker*. Comic ballet *Coppélia*, which we see
Vicky performing, features a dancing doll, manipulated by a sinister
Svengali, Dr Coppélius. Another comic ballet, Massine's *La Boutique
fantasque*, also shown in the film, stages a violent revolution in a
toyshop when two of the dancing dolls are separated from each
other. The Archers retold a version of the Coppélia story in *The
Tales of Hoffmann*. In Jacques Offenbach's telling, the doll, Olympia
(played by Shearer), is brought to life but then viciously destroyed
by Coppélius. Key to Olympia/Coppélia's eerie appearance are her
enamel eyes. We first see Vicky with her eyes hidden by tiny opera
glasses, creating a similar effect, and the scene from the ballet shown

Vicky plays Coppélia
(Photograph by
Alistair Phillips)

in the film is of her learning to blink. Vicky and The Girl are each other's doppelgänger, with dangerously linked destinies. Boris steps surely into this Svengali role and talks about 'making' a great dancer out of Vicky.

Considering the film's legacy in ballet horror, we can draw a line from *The Red Shoes* to the doppelgänger theme, madness and dance-specific body horror in *Black Swan*. Also too, the idea that the ballet company's discipline and eerie beauty radiates from one monstrous source in *Suspiria*. However, the incarnadine palette and Expressionist architecture of Argento's film demonstrate that the legacy of *The Red Shoes* is as aesthetic as thematic. Powell finds horror even in the visuals of a romantic ballet and Charles Garnier's ornate architecture for the Opéra de Monte-Carlo. A dissolve from Vicky's *attitude* pose in the *pas de deux* of *Les Sylphides* matches her shape perfectly with the winged cherub atop a gargoyle outside Boris's Monte-Carlo office. As Michael Williams points out in his essay on Walbrook, the gargoyle mirrors Boris's essentially monstrous nature,[122] to which Vicky dances ever closer.

The prevalence of enchanted female figures in ballets resonates with the predicament of Karen/The Girl, forced to dance against her will, her body controlled by another force. It also feeds into the idea of Vicky being manipulated by Boris, via his creation and management of her career, in return for which he expects total loyalty. She is likewise controlled, to a certain extent, by Julian's music, which she must always follow. Vicky becomes an uncanny version of herself, a doll form, manipulated by external forces, which ultimately transport her to her death. All three women (Karen/The Girl/Vicky) have something in common with the zombie: bodies animated by magic. Surely it is no coincidence that *The Tales of Hoffmann* inspired George A. Romero to make movies. There is something undead, or at least uncanny, about the airtight, studio-bound ideal of the composed film: predetermined steps taken in a rigorously defined space to a relentless rhythm, without room for the improvisation, variation, accident or individual expression.

Vicky surrounded by monsters

Apt then that the figures who encircle Vicky and lift her into the spotlight appear to be zombies: half-decomposed, and easily led, with bones and guts protruding from their faces. The masks were designed by Heckroth and made by Terence Morgan II, decorated with 'ghostly hands, devil's horns, weird insects, spiders' webs and birds' nests made in plastic and trimmed with hair, beads and scraps of lace'.[123] The horrific aspect of the ballerina in *The Red Shoes* is not simply physical – the revelation that there is a sweating, bleeding, dying body in the shape of the hyper-feminine, impossibly light dancer. The horror of *The Red Shoes* is pre-eminently psychological. Vicky must dance with her demons to achieve greatness.

7 Coda: 'Doubtful comforts'

Vicky's dressing room in Monte-Carlo: Boris and Julian face each
other again over a ballerina's body. Except this is not the cast of a
foot, but the living Vicky, who is due on stage shortly. Two things
are wrong with this picture: she is wearing the red shoes, and she is
in floods of tears. Boris is in evening dress and Julian wears his long
leather coat – he has fled here from Covent Garden and the first night
of his new opera. In the mirror, the figures of the two men merge:
Boris's head on Julian's body.

***

Almost every time I told someone I was writing about *The Red Shoes*,
they gasped at the sound of its name. The film's memory inspires in
many a rush of simultaneous delight and agony. It is a dangerous
film to watch at an impressionable age. Feminist novelist Margaret
Atwood was one of many young viewers to be entranced by the film,
but on first viewing she instantly absorbed the idea that a woman
can never be allowed to be a great artist. '*The Red Shoes* syndrome'
was something to be resisted. In the 1980s, a student at the American
Ballet School told writer Suzanne Gordon that she was 'so moved
and terrified by Moira Shearer's tragic end that she said she would
never think of taking up with a man'. But is Vicky's real choice simply
between submitting to the demands of her husband and those of her
vocation? Can a film so fascinating have such a blunt and regressive
message? Would Powell and Pressburger, whose heroines are so
noble, quick-witted, modern and self-reliant, have offered us a Vicky
Page, only to let her bleed out on the altar of the patriarchy?

Sue Harper scorns readings of *The Red Shoes*'s ending as an
endorsement of 'the excision of those females who aspired to the status
of artists, and that the blood on the ballet shoes symbolized the author's

Boris and Julian merge as they fight for Vicky

desire that women return to an essential, menstrual femininity'.[124] The Archers' sexual politics are essentially bohemian, the Ballet Lermontov is composed of happy singletons, and if *The Red Shoes* has a message, she argues, it is that it was 'family life, with its suffocatingly mean horizons, which rang the death knell of creativity'.[125] Andrew Moor discovers a 'site of radical resistance'[126] in the Ballet Lermontov, which opposes heteronormative conventions, and emphasises the film's 'blatantly homosexual origins'.[127] That goes back to both Hans Christian Andersen and the affair between Diaghilev and Nijinsky as recounted by Nijinsky's wife, as well as to Walbrook's portrayal of Lermontov and Massine's camp Grischa. In Romola's memoirs she reports Diaghilev equating genius with a rejection of heteronormativity. The older man believed that: 'almost all great geniuses in the past were homosexual, or at least bisexual,' and that 'love between the same sex, even if the persons involved are quite ordinary, because of the very similarity of their natures and the absence of presupposed difference, is creative and artistic'.[128] The Nijinsky–Diaghilev love triangle is reconfigured as both heterosexual and asexual in the film; the love between Julian and Vicky is innocent (and conventional), and Boris is jealous of Vicky 'in a way that you [Julian] will never understand'. If ballet, in Richard Dyer's words, offers queer viewers a vision of heterosexual love 'so ethereally idealized that it becomes rather unreal … the spectacle of heterosexuality paraded as glittering illusion',[129] then *The Red Shoes* undermines the idea of marriage as a happy ending. It does this partly by portraying a supposed love triangle that is only an illusion of romance. The real drama is more deadly, and the life of a bohemian artist also has its perils. The Ballet Lermontov is 'a men's club of collaborative artists,' writes Alexander Doty, but one that 'vitally depended upon women – or at least one woman per project'.[130] Vicky is elevated but also objectified by Lermontov's mentorship. Moor argues that the ballet's looming darknesses represent how 'women can be annihilated in an unforgiving and unsatisfactory masculine system'.[131] So the film's ending doesn't just ask the audience if they want to dance like Vicky, to die for art, but also, in Doty's words, asks 'gay and queerly positioned aesthetes who have some expressive investment in straight women to reconsider their position'.[132]

Vicky's shared understanding with Boris, I would argue, is that she, like him, is prepared to embrace her demons, to be raised up by her monsters. She is prepared, in his words, to ignore her human nature, to repress her sexuality, even if she cannot alter it. She is listening when Boris explains to Grischa backstage at *Giselle* that 'The dancer who relies upon the doubtful comforts of human love will never be a great dancer. Never.' He turns his head towards her as he talks, she turns her head back to listen, before taking to the stage as one of the Wilis, ghosts of wronged women who take lethal revenge on men. A whip pan and a cut from Boris's declaration that human nature is best ignored takes us to the station, where the Ballet Lermontov luggage is addressed to Monte-Carlo; such ruthlessness is the engine that drives this company. The egotism of artists becomes a

Backstage, Vicky listens as Boris delivers a speech for her benefit

running joke: Grischa demands the spotlight 'toujours sur moi', and Irina is constantly late. But there is a deeper truth to such vanity: the selfishness required to dedicate one's life to a solitary artistic pursuit. Boris 'has no heart', Vicky embodies a mechanical creature with a demonic face, who lives to dance, not to love.

Vicky's monstrousness is more shocking than Boris's because she is a woman. Women, as Jenny Offill explores in her novel *Dept. of Speculation*, are conditioned to become selfless wives instead of selfish monsters. 'My plan was to never get married,' her heroine counters. 'I was going to be an art monster instead. Women almost never become art monsters because art monsters only concern themselves with art, never mundane things. Nabokov didn't even fold his umbrella. Véra licked his stamps for him.'[133] Offill's twenty-first-century heroine gets married, has a child, and so never writes her second novel. In the 1940s, this pressure to choose marriage

Vicky and Boris:
dying for art
(Photograph by
Alistair Phillips)

over work was more overt for all women who contemplated a career
whether because of their natural talents, or because their horizons
had been widened by the opportunities briefly afforded them during
wartime. For decades, women were routinely expected to give up
work after marriage, as Shearer and Diana Gould did. Vicky finds
herself a husband who composes operas,[134] rather than licks stamps.
He can't support her in her career. Yet her destiny as a ballerina is
set in motion the moment that she meets Boris and tells him that she
needs to dance as she needs to live; it is sealed when he sees her dance
with passion and perfectionism at a matinée. In that moment of eye
contact, he recognises her monstrous capacity.

Vicky struggles, at the last moment, to become fully monstrous.
It is not a question of whether she loves Julian, but of whether she is

prepared to leave him for ballet. Of degrees of selfishness. For female artists, the question that counts, as Claire Dederer writes, is: '*What if I'm not monster enough?*' Female artists don't have to leave their spouses, but they do need to 'abandon *something*, some nurturing part' of themselves[135] – the part that cares about the life that stands between a woman and a world tour, a masterpiece, a finished manuscript. To lock the office door, to attend auditions instead of birthday dinners, rehearsals instead of school plays. To hire and fire composers without sentiment, to laugh when an employee resigns in a rage. To be like Posy Fossil, who kills the 'nice qualities' in herself to further her art. Or Karen, who leaves the old woman to die alone while she dances. Shearer always called ballet a selfish career. To be an art monster is to find fulfilment outside 'the doubtful comforts of human love' – 'to go out and die for art'. Julian will always lose Vicky, not least because he proves hopelessly un-monstrous when he walks away from his own opening night to save his marriage. 'Why didn't you?' he asks. He knows why. He succeeds only in weakening her resolve – then the shoes take their vengeance. Powell's best description of the film is as 'a haunting, insolent picture, in the way it takes for granted that nothing matters but art, and that art is something worth dying for'.[136] He wrote those words when describing his interactions with de Valois. They couldn't agree on much, but he sensed they agreed on this final point: 'but [she] only applied it to her little world'.

Boris is not a composite of Diaghilev, Korda, Powell and Pressburger. He represents a trait all such creative figures must share: the egotistical capacity for selfishness. Even Vicky. He is the undiluted art monster, who lives only for creativity and will turn on a former protégée the moment their loyalty is divided. The horror of *The Red Shoes*, for this viewer, is the recognition of this monstrousness within oneself. When the final performance of *The Red Shoes* ends, intercut with Julian removing the shoes from Vicky's feet, Boris's head falls back, his mouth opens. The speech he makes that night is rasping and almost robotic. He has lost something, a fragment of his humanity, leaving him a truly heartless monster. Vicky's tragedy is

Boris announces
Vicky's death to
the audience

his catharsis too – and ours. Didn't we want Vicky to keep on
dancing? The candle that was freshly lit in the film's first title card
has now sputtered out. If the film is a tragedy, as so many ballet
narratives are, Vicky is undone by her weakness, but her ambition is
a seductive vice, one that glows with the blood-red vibrancy of satin
ribbons on a brand-new pair of shoes.

Many artists have answered the film's challenge. British ballet
movie *Billy Elliot* (Stephen Daldry, 2000) features a shot mimicking
the transformation scene in the red shoes ballet, with a pair of shoes
thrown down at Billy's feet. 'Go on, I dare you,' says the teacher off-
camera. Martin Scorsese, long vocal about his passion for *The Red
Shoes*, and dedicated in his support of his restoration, emphasised
the monstrous side of the protagonist in *Raging Bull* (1980). Jake
La Motta (Robert De Niro) has a capacity for explosive violence
that leads him to victory in the boxing ring, even while it destroys
his family. And yet he laces up his red gloves again and again, just
as Vicky answers Boris's sibilant, serpent call: 'put on the red shoes'.
Joanna Hogg's *The Souvenir* diptych (2019 and 2021) employs
imagery and takes inspiration from *The Red Shoes* as her protagonist
Julie (Honor Swinton Byrne) learns to work through her personal
tragedy, reject interference and fight for her own film-making voice.

On stage, the Broadway musical adaptation was a notorious flop in 1993, but ballet has fared better. Ballet Ireland's 2005 production *Diaghilev and The Red Shoes* incorporates the central ballet in a tribute to the impresario. Despite not using Easdale's score, Matthew Bourne's 2016 interpretation of the story remixes the film's themes and aesthetic to stunning effect – it is best enjoyed by those who have already seen and loved the film. In music, Kate Bush drew on *The Red Shoes* for a 1993 song with violent, urgent lyrics about voodoo and divas, and an album of the same name, as well as a short film, *The Line, the Cross and the Curve* (also 1993), incorporating the feature's imagery. Her words echo the blood-soaked lines of Anne Sexton's poem of 1972, 'The Red Shoes', in which the footwear represents ambition handed down from mother to daughter 'hidden like shameful letters'. In Sexton's poem: 'All those girls / Who wore the red shoes, / Each boarded a train that would not stop.'[137]

Powell included *The Red Shoes* ballet in a proposed series of filmed ballets in the early 1960s: each one was chosen to illustrate 'the Ballet's connection with revolutionary movements in Art which were taking place at that period (unperceived by the general public) which sometimes shocked, horrified or puzzled the critics of the day, but have since become Big Business'.[138] After failing to impress the Rank executives and horrifying many critics, *The Red Shoes* became 'Big Business': the biggest film at the US box office in 1948. Its continued relevance and centrality to film culture vindicate the ambitious, insolent vision of The Archers. The duo refused permission for adaptations, remakes and sequels, but did collaborate in 1977 on a novelisation of the film – partly in the hope that they could make more money from their biggest hit.

* * *

Perhaps you disagree with my take on *The Red Shoes*. We may need to rid ourselves of the idea that the film has a message at all. If ever a film represented art for art's sake, it is this one. It is a manifesto for creativity and excellence even in a time of austerity and uncertainty.

The film can be appreciated as an experiment in film, as dance, as animated painting – and as a backstage melodrama that brought a new darkness to the genre. The collaborative nature of the film and its long production history make room for a variety of voices, and arguments, and the empty spotlight in the film's finale suggests a question, not a solution. The ambition of its vision, and the emphasis on enchantment and psychological turmoil, raise *The Red Shoes* to the status of a new myth, one as fascinating and as open to interpretation as Andersen's tale.

The film takes the form of a challenge, one we all respond to in different degrees: how far would you go for art? The icon of that challenge is the pair of red satin dancing slippers, handed to the audience in the knowledge that they cannot resist them. That's why so many children left the cinema clamouring for dance lessons. It is also why the film still fascinates, 75 years after its release. The lure of *The Red Shoes* remains potent.

A challenge to the audience

Notes

1 All quotations from the Andersen story are taken from the 'New translation by Alan Welton' included in the press dossier for *The Red Shoes*, titled 'Information Folder', held in Special Collections, BFI National Archive. The original Danish tale was first published on 7 April 1845 in a volume titled *Nye Eventyr. Første Bind. Tredie Samling* or *New Fairy Tales. First Volume. Third Collection.*

2 And her crimson compact, dress and shoes, which she carries but does not wear.

3 Laura Mulvey, *Death 24x a Second: Stillness and the Moving Image* (London: Reaktion Books, 2006), p. 76.

4 When Pavlova died, in accordance with ballet tradition, her company performed the next show with her role replaced by a spotlight, as the Ballet Lermontov does after Vicky's death in *The Red Shoes*.

5 Erin Mackie, 'Red Shoes and Bloody Stumps', in Shari Benstock and Suzanne Ferriss (eds), *Footnotes: On Shoes* (New Brunswick, NJ and London: Rutgers University Press, 2001), p. 246.

6 Michael Powell, *A Life in Movies: An Autobiography* (London: Heinemann, 1986), p. 611.

7 Mackie, 'Red Shoes and Bloody Stumps', p. 245.

8 Mara Mandradjieff, 'Ballerina-pointe Shoe Becoming, Fluid Multiplicities, and *The Red Shoes*', *Text and Performance Quarterly*, vol. 36, no. 4 (2016), p. 268.

9 Ibid., p. 267.

10 Ian Christie, 'Blood-red Shoes?', in Elizabeth Ezra and Catherine Wheatley (eds), *Shoe Reels: The History and Philosophy of Footwear in Film* (Edinburgh: Edinburgh University Press, 2021), p. 76.

11 Linda Ruth Williams, 'The Shock of *The Red Shoes*', *New Review of Film and Television Studies*, vol. 15, no. 1 (23 February 2017), p. 11.

12 F. Maurice Speed, 'The Screen', *What's On in London*, 23 July 1948, p. 7.

13 C. A. Lejeune, 'In Love with Ballet', *Observer*, 25 July 1948, p. 2.

14 Milton Shulman, 'So This Is Covent Garden (Or Is It?)', *Evening Standard*, 23 July 1948, p. 6.

15 Ann Slavit, The Red Shoes at BAM, 2013. Available at: <aslavit.myportfolio.com/the-red-shoes-at-bam> (accessed 29 September 2022).

16 Evelyn Webber, 'High-price Film (It's British It's Ballet) Sets Record', *Daily Express*, 18 November 1950, p. 5.

17 Some sources say the shoes were red.

18 Quoted, Kevin Macdonald, *Emeric Pressburger: The Life and Death of a Screenwriter* (London and Boston, MA: Faber and Faber, 1994), p. 9.

19 Judith Mackrell, *Bloomsbury Ballerina: Lydia Lopokova, Imperial Dancer and Mrs John Maynard Keynes* (London and Phoenix, AZ: Orion, 2013), p. 342.

20 Information Folder, Special Collections, BFI National Archive.

21 Powell, *A Life in Movies*, p. 121.

22 Ibid.

23 Michael Powell, *Million-Dollar Movie: The Second Volume of His Life in Movies* (London: Heinemann, 1992), p. 61.

24 Thelma Schoonmaker, interview with the author, 2017.

25 Macdonald, *Emeric Pressburger*, p. 58.

26 Powell, *A Life in Movies*, p. 113.

27 Powell had met Duncan in Cap-Ferrat in 1921.

28 All quotations from G. B. Stern, *A Pair of Red Shoes*, Special Collections, BFI National Archive.

29 Quoted, Macdonald, *Emeric Pressburger*, pp. 275–6.

30 Romola Nijinsky's biography was finally filmed by Herbert Ross in 1980 as *Nijinsky*, starring Alan Bates as Diaghilev and ballet dancer George de la Peña as Vaslav Nijinsky.

31 Harrison was the UK manager of Technicolor Ltd.

32 Quoted, Macdonald, *Emeric Pressburger*, p. 278.

33 Powell, *A Life in Movies*, pp. 613–14.

34 Ibid., p. 614.

35 Ibid.

36 Tom White correspondence, 24 January 1947, Special Collections, BFI National Archive.

37 Ibid., 4 February 1947.

38 Vicky is playing Odette at the end of Act II, but the music is very fast.

39 Powell, *A Life in Movies*, p. 305.

40 Powell, *Million-Dollar Movie*, p. 156.

41 Ibid.

42 Speech by Michael Powell in 1980, quoted in Ian Christie, *Arrows of Desire: The Films of Michael Powell and Emeric Pressburger*, 2nd edn (London: Faber and Faber, 1994), p. 19.

43 Powell, *Million-Dollar Movie*, p. 154.

44 Powell, *A Life in Movies*, p. 651.

45 Ibid.

46 Ibid., p. 652.

47 Ian Christie, 'Another Life in Movies: Pressburger and Powell', in Ian Christie and Andrew Moor (eds), *The Cinema of Michael Powell: International Perspectives on an English Film-maker* (London: BFI, 2005), p. 181.

48 Quoted, ibid., pp. 189–90.

49 The Archers functioned as a production unit with relative autonomy, as members of the Independent Producers system under the umbrella of the Rank Organisation.

50 Powell, *A Life in Movies*, p. 624.

51 Quoted, Macdonald, *Emeric Pressburger*, p. 284.

52 Jack Cardiff, *Magic Hour* (London: Faber and Faber, 1997), pp. 90–1.

53 Although in his memoir *Magic Hour*, he does recall weeping after seeing Pavlova perform *The Dying Swan* in a music hall when he was a child.

54 Powell, *A Life in Movies*, p. 653.

55 Screenplay for *The Red Shoes*, dated 1947, file S4205, Special Collections, BFI National Archive.

56 Remade in 1940, after the enforcement of the Hays Code, with Vivien Leigh in the lead role – and far more ballet and less sex work than in the original.

57 *Billy Elliot* (Stephen Daldry, 2000), probably British cinema's second most-beloved ballet film, picks up this baton: its hero is a boy living in a pit village during the Miners' Strike, excluded by default from the world of ballet by prejudices around class, gender and sexuality.

58 Baffling as such shops would not sell ballet shoes.

59 The sleepy speech Julian delivers in the carriage to Vicky, beginning, 'One day when I'm old …' is here given to Vicky.

60 A later screenplay for *The Red Shoes*, file S4204, Special Collections, BFI National Archive.

61 Powell, *A Life in Movies*, p. 583.

62 Charles Barr, 'The First Four Minutes', in Christie and Moor, *The Cinema of Michael Powell*, p. 32.

63 Powell, *A Life in Movies*, p. 583.

64 Richard Winnington, 'Less in This Film Than Meets the Eye', *News Chronicle*, 19 April 1951, p. 3.

65 Powell, *A Life in Movies*, p. 583.

66 Arnold Haskell, 'The Birth of the English Ballet', *Journal of the Royal Society of Arts*, vol. 87, no. 4517 (16 June 1939), p. 785.

67 Léonide Massine, *My Life in Ballet*, (eds) Phyllis Hartnoll and Robert Rubens (London: Macmillan and New York: St. Martin's Press, 1968), p. 63.

68 Ibid., pp. 62–3.

69 Caryl Brahms, 'Massine's Return', *Tempo*, no. 4 (Summer 1947), p. 22.

70 Quoted, Macdonald, *Emeric Pressburger*, pp. 279–80.

71 Sergei Eisenstein, *Notes of a Film Director* (Moscow: Foreign Languages Publishing House, 1946), p. 5.

72 Hein Heckroth, 'Colour Film My Medium of Expression', *Daily Film Renter*, 19 April 1951, p. 15.

73 Mark Nicholls, 'A Group Marriage without Sex: Fusion and Collaboration in The Archers' *The Red Shoes* (1948)', *Journal of Film and Video*, vol. 70, no. 1 (Spring 2018), p. 46.

74 Born Józef Żmigrod in Tarnów, then part of Austria-Hungary.

75 In the German film industry, where he started work, he had scored *Emil and the Detectives* (Gerhard Lamprecht, 1931), which Pressburger co-wrote.

76 Hein Heckroth's diary, 17 March 1947, quoted, Macdonald, *Emeric Pressburger*, p. 284.

77 Powell, *A Life in Movies*, pp. 626–7.

78 Ibid., p. 628.

79 Ibid., pp. 630–1.

80 Michael Powell, 'The Ballet of The Red Shoes', Special Collections, BFI National Archive.

81 Cardiff, *Magic Hour*, p. 95.

82 Herb Lightman, 'The Red Shoes', *American Cinematographer*, vol. 30, no. 3 (March 1949), p. 83.

83 Massine, *My Life in Ballet*, p. 232.

84 £10,000, double what Goring and Page were on apiece, and nearly as much as Walbrook at £12,000, though the others did accrue some overtime.

85 Powell, *A Life in Movies*, p. 631.

86 Quoted, Macdonald, *Emeric Pressburger*, p. 286.

87 Hortense Powdermaker, *Hollywood: The Dream Factory – An Anthropologist Looks at the Movie Makers* (London: Secker & Warburg, 1950), p. 98.

88 Powell, *A Life in Movies*, p. 640.

89 Powell, *Million-Dollar Movie*, p. 279.

90 During production of *The Red Shoes*, Goring was 35, and Shearer 21.

91 Powell, *A Life in Movies*, p. 644.

92 Caryl Brahms, 'About the Ballet', *Good Housekeeping* (February 1944), p. 40.

93 Ninette de Valois, *Step by Step: The Formation of an Establishment* (London: W. H. Allen, 1977), p. 189.

94 By actors Julia Lang and Bill Shine, who were married at the time.

95 Noel Streatfeild, *Ballet Shoes* (London: Dent, 1936), p. 214.

96 Haskell, 'The Birth of the English Ballet', p. 802.

97 Moira Shearer, interviews with Dale Harris 1976–8, Jerome Robbins Dance Division collections, New York Public Library, p. 192.

98 Ibid., p. 146.

99 Peter Craig-Raymond, 'The Career of Moira Shearer', *Ballet Today*, December 1954, p. 19.

100 Barbara Newman, *Striking a Balance: Dancers Talk about Dancing* (London: Elm Tree Books, 1982), p. 97.

101 Elizabeth Salter, *Helpmann: The Authorised Biography* (New York: Universe Books, 1978), p. 139.

102 Arlene Croce, *Afterimages* (New York: Vintage Books, 1979), p. 439.

103 Shearer, interviews with Dale Harris, p. 213.

104 Lee Edward Stern, 'How It Really Is in the Dance World', *New York Times*, 18 November 1979, p. 14.

105 Roger Wood 'Some Opinions on "The Red Shoes" (Film)', *Ballet*, vol. 5, no. 8 (August–September 1948). Available at: <https://powell-pressburger.org/Reviews/48_TRS/Critics.html> (accessed 1 February 2023).

106 Quoted, Karen Eliot, *Dancing Lives: Five Female Dancers from the Ballet d'Action to Merce Cunningham* (Urbana and Chicago: University of Illinois Press, 2007), p. 95.

107 Screenplay for *The Red Shoes*, dated 1947, file S4205, Special Collections, BFI National Archive.

108 Michael Powell and Emeric Pressburger, *The Red Shoes: The Classic Story* (New York: Avon Books, 1978), p. 3.

109 Ibid. A direct reference surely to English dancer Hilda Munnings who changed her name to Lydia Sokolova on joining the Ballets Russes in 1913.

110 Adrienne L. McLean, '"The Red Shoes" Revisited', *Dance Chronicle*, vol. 11, no. 1 (1988), p. 42.

111 Croce, *Afterimages*, p. 440.

112 Andrew Moor, *Powell and Pressburger: A Cinema of Magic Spaces* (London: I. B. Tauris, 2012), p. 198.

113 Dilys Powell, 'Films of the Week', *Sunday Times*, 25 July 1948, p. 2.

114 Lejeune, 'In Love with Ballet', p. 2.

115 Monk Gibbon, *The Red Shoes: A Critical Study* (London: Saturn Press, 1948), p. 78.

116 Legendary Hollywood choreographer who had also worked as a dancer and choreographer for Ballets Russes de Monte-Carlo by this point.

117 Lisa Duffy, 'Fantasy Spaces of Hollywood Dance Musicals 1940–1960: Explorations of Gender and Sexuality', unpublished doctoral thesis, 2019, p. 62.

118 Cardiff, *Magic Hour*, p. 94.

119 Moor, *Powell and Pressburger*, p. 198.

120 Katharina Lindner, *Film Bodies: Queer Feminist Encounters with Gender and Sexuality in Cinema* (London: I. B. Tauris, 2022), p. 80.

121 *The Dying Swan* (Yevgeni Bauer, 1917), starring the Russian ballet dancer Vera Karalli.

122 Michael Williams, 'Anton Walbrook: The Continental Consort', in Tim Bergfelder and Christian Cargnelli (eds), *Destination London: German-speaking Emigrés and British Cinema, 1925–1950* (New York and Oxford: Berghahn Books, 2008), p. 160.

123 Press book, Special Collections, BFI National Archive.

124 Sue Harper, 'From *Holiday Camp* to High Camp: Women in British Feature Films, 1945–1951', in Andrew Higson (ed.), *Dissolving Views: Key Writings on British Cinema* (London: Bloomsbury, 2016), p. 109.

125 Ibid., p. 110.

126 Andrew Moor, 'Bending the Arrow: The Queer Appeal of the Archers', in Christie and Moor, *Michael Powell*, p. 218.

127 Ibid., p. 219.

128 Romola Nijinsky, *Nijinsky and The Last Years of Nijinsky* (London: Victor Gollancz, 1980), pp. 109–10.

129 Richard Dyer, *Only Entertainment* (London and New York: Routledge, 1992), p. 12.

130 Alexander Doty, 'The Queer Aesthete, the Diva, and *The Red Shoes*', *Flaming Classics: Queering the Film Canon* (London and New York: Routledge, 2000), p. 112.

131 Moor, *Powell and Pressburger*, p. 217.

132 Ibid.

133 Jenny Offill, *Dept. of Speculation* (London: Granta, 2015), p. 8.

134 His opera, *Cupid and Psyche*, is itself a mythical story about a woman torn between the worlds of men and gods.

135 Claire Dederer, 'What Do We Do with the Art of Monstrous Men?', *Paris Review*, 20 November 2017. Available at: <www.theparisreview.org/blog/2017/11/20/art-monstrous-men/> (accessed 29 September 2022).

136 Powell, *A Life in Movies*, p. 660.

137 Anne Sexton, 'The Red Shoes', *The Book of Folly* (Boston, MA: Houghton Mifflin, 1972), p. 28.

138 Michael Powell, Proposal for 'The Art of Ballet from "Scheherazade" to "The Red Shoes" (1910–1962)', Special Collections, BFI National Archive.

Credits

The Red Shoes
UK
1948

J. Arthur Rank presents
A production of
The Archers
© 1948 Independent
Producers

**Written, Produced
and Directed by**
Michael Powell
Emeric Pressburger
Original Screenplay by
Emeric Pressburger
Based on the story by
Hans Christian Andersen
Additional Dialogue
Keith Winter
Director of Photography
Jack Cardiff A.S.C.
Camera
Christopher Challis
Colour Control
Natalie Kalmus
Associate
Joan Bridge
Scenic Artist
Alfred Roberts
Special Painting
Ivor Beddoes
Józef Natanson
**Technicolor Composite
Photography**
F. George Gunn
Eugene Hague
(as E. Hague)
Editor
Reginald Mills

Sound
Charles Poulton
Dubbing
Gordon K. McCallum
(as Gordon MacCullum)
Music Recorder
Ted Drake
Liaison Editor
John Seabourne Jr
Continuity
Doreen North
Wardrobe
Dorothy Edwards
Assistant Producer
George R. Busby
Assistant Director
Sydney S. Streeter
**Miss Shearer's Dresses
by**
Jacques Fath of Paris
Mattli of London
**Mlle Tcherina's Dresses
by**
Carven of Paris
**Music Composed
and Arranged by**
Brian Easdale
Music Played by
The Royal Philharmonic
Orchestra
Aria Sung by
Margherita Grandi
**Café de Paris Sequence
Music**
Ted Heath's Kenny Baker
Swing Group
Production Designed by
Hein Heckroth
Art Director
Arthur Lawson

**Choreography – The
Ballet of The Red Shoes**
Robert Helpmann
**The Part of the
Shoemaker Created
and Danced by**
Leonide Massine
**Conductor – The Royal
Philharmonic Orchestra**
Sir Thomas Beecham,
Bart.

uncredited

Make-up Artists
George Blackler
Eric Carter
Ernest Gasser
**Third Assistant
Directors**
J. M. Gibson
Laurie Knight
**Second Assistant
Director**
Kenneth K. Rick
Draughtsmen
Bernard Goodwin
G. Heavens
Don Picton
V. Shaw
V. B. Wilkins
Alan Withy
Scenic Painter
Peter Mullins
Assistant Art Director
Elven Webb
Boom Operator
Al Burton
**First Assistant Dubbing
Mixer**
Peter Davies

Sound Recordist
Desmond Dew
Dubbing Editor
Leonard Trumm
Matte Artists
Les Bowie
Judy Jordan
Still Photographer
George Cannon
Clapper Loaders
Bob Kindred
John Morgan
Special Still
Photographer
Cornel Lucas
Focus Puller
George Minassian
Assistant Still
Photographer
Alistair Phillips
Chief Electrician
Bill Wall
Head of Wardrobe
Elsie Withers
Assistant Editor
Noreen Ackland
Additional Editing
Bert Bates
Second Editor
Anne V. Coates
Second Assistant
Editors
Tony Haynes
Laurie Knight
Assistant Continuity
Joanna Busby
Production Assistant
Gwladys Jenks
Publicist
Vivienne Knight

Production Secretary
Marjorie Mein
Mask Maker
Terence Morgan II
Production Assistant
Charles Orme

CAST
Anton Walbrook
Boris Lermontov
Marius Goring
Julian Craster
Moira Shearer
Victoria Page
Robert Helpmann
Ivan Boleslawsky
Léonide Massine
(as Leonide Massine)
Grischa Ljubov
Albert Bassermann
(as Albert Basserman)
Sergei Ratov
Esmond Knight
Livy
Jean Short
Terry
Gordon Littmann
Ike
Julia Lang
a balletomane
Bill Shine
her mate
Austin Trevor
Professor Palmer
Eric Berry
Dimitri
Irene Browne
Lady Neston
Ludmilla Tchérina
(as Ludmilla Tcherina)
Irina Boronskaja

Jerry Verno
stage-door keeper
Derek Elphinstone
Lord Oldham
Marie Rambert
(as Madame Rambert)
Madame Rambert
Joy Rawlins
Gwladys (Vicky's friend)
Marcel Poncin
M. Boudin
Michel Bazalgette
M. Rideaut
Yvonne Andre
Vicky's dresser
Hay Petrie
Boisson
Alan Carter
Joan Harris
solo dancers and
assistants maîtres de
ballet – The Ballet of
The Red Shoes
Joan Sheldon
Paula Dunning
Brian Ashbridge
Denis Carey
Lynne Dorval
Helen Ffrance
Robert Dorning
Eddie Gaillard
Paul Hammond
Tommy Linden
Trisha Linova
Anna Marinova
Guy Massey
John Regan
Peggy Sager
Ruth Sendler
dancers – The Ballet of
The Red Shoes

Hilda Gaunt
accompanist – The Ballet
of The Red Shoes

uncredited
Neville Astor
Edmond Audran
Mark Baring
Michael Bayston
Leonard Boucher
Anne Byatt
Joy Camden
Jack Carter
Elizabeth Christie
Peter Fisk
Gladys Forrester
Donato Forte
Greta Grayson
Audrey Harman
Pamela Harrington
Suzanne Jemmett
Barry Klare
Joan Lehman
Joyce Linden
Charles Lisner
Graham MacCormack
Enid Martin
Denise Merrum
Helene Mladova

Patricia Norman
Yvonne Olena
Collin Patrick
Philippe Perrottet
Jackie Smithers
Saxon Stobart
Margaret Tate
Meta Thomas
John Tore
Gladys Walton
Anne Woolliams
Marnia Zarina
corps de ballet
Peter Bayliss
Evans – Lord Oldham's
chauffeur
Robin Burns
Mercury Theatre
audience
Michelle de Lys
Lady in Vicky's dressing
room before premiere
Jane Fischer
dancer
Richard George
doorman
Jean Hébey
Parisian taxi driver at
Opera Square

Leslie Phillips
audience member
Emeric Pressburger
man waiting on station
platform
Patrick Troughton
BBC radio announcer
(voice)
Elizabeth West
Lermontov's secretary
George Woodbridge
doorman – Covent
Garden

Production Details
35mm
1.37:1
Colour (Technicolor)
Running time:
136 minutes

Release Details
UK theatrical release
on 6 September 1948 by
General Film Distributors
US theatrical release
on 21 October 1948 by
Eagle-Lion Films